Josef Hofmann.

Josef Hofmann

PIANO PLAYING

WITH

PIANO QUESTIONS ANSWERED

With a New Introduction by
GREGOR BENKO
President, International Piano Archives

DOVER PUBLICATIONS, INC. NEW YORK

Published in Canada by General Publishing Company, Ltd., 30 Lesmill Road, Don Mills, Toronto, Ontario.

Published in the United Kingdom by Constable and Company, Ltd.

This Dover edition, first published in 1976, is an unabridged and unaltered republication of the work as published in 1920. Gregor Benko has written a new Introduction especially for the Dover edition.

International Standard Book Number: 0-486-23362-6
Library of Congress Catalog Card Number: 76-19515

Manufactured in the United States of America
Dover Publications, Inc.
180 Varick Street
New York, N.Y. 10014

Piano Questions Answered

CONTENTS

CONTENTS

A FOREWORD

THIS little book is compiled from the questions and my answers to them, as they have appeared during the past two years in the *Ladies' Home Journal.* Since the questions came mostly from young piano students and cover a large number of matters important to the study of the piano, it was thought that this republication might be of interest to piano students in general, and that, gathered into a little volume, they might form a new and perhaps not unwelcome sort of reference book.

To serve as such and to facilitate the reader's search for any particular subject, I have grouped the questions, together with their answers, under special headings.

It is only natural, however, that a book of this character cannot contain more than mere suggestions to stimulate the reader's individual thinking. Positive facts, which can be found in books on musical history and in kindred works, are, therefore, stated only where they are needful as a basis for the replies. Any rule or advice given to some particular person cannot fit every other person unless it is passed through the sieve of one's own individual intelligence and is, by this process, so modified as to fit one's own particular case.

There are, in addition to the questions presented and answered, one or two points about piano-playing that would naturally not occur to the average student. The opportunity to discuss those here is too favourable to be allowed to pass, and as they hardly admit of precise classification, I venture to offer them here as a brief foreword.

To the hundreds of students who at various times have asked me: What is the quickest way to become a great piano-player? I will say that such a thing as a royal road, a secret trick, or a patent method to quickly become a great artist, does not exist. As the world consists of atoms; as it is the infinitely small things that have forced the microscope into the scientist's hand, so does art contain numberless small, seemingly insignificant things

A FOREWORD

which, if neglected entirely, visit dire vengeance upon the student. Instead of prematurely concerning himself with his inspiration, spirituality, genius, fancy, etc., and neglecting on their account the material side of piano study, the student should be willing to progress from atom to atom, slowly, deliberately, but with absolute certainty that each problem has been completely solved, each difficulty fully overcome, before he faces the next one. Leaps, there are none!

Unquestionably it does sometimes happen that an artist suddenly acquires a wide renown. In such a case his leap was not into greatness, but merely into the public's recognition of it; the greatness must have been in him for some time before the public became aware of it. If there was any leaping, it was not the artist, but the public that did it.

Let us not close our eyes to the fact that there have been — and probably always will be — artists that gain a wide renown *without* being great; puffery, aided by some personal eccentricity, is quite able to mislead the public, but these will, at best, do it only for a short time, and the collapse of such a reputation, as collapse there must be, is always sure, and sad to behold.

The buoyancy of mind, its ability to soar, so necessary for both creative and interpretative art, these are never impaired by close attention to detail. If they should be destroyed by attention to detail, it would not matter, for they cannot have been genuine; they can have been but sentimental imaginings. Details are the very steps which, one by one, lead to the summit of art; we should be careful not to lift one foot before the other one rests quite securely upon its step. One should — to illustrate — not be satisfied with the ability of "getting through" some difficult passage "by the skin of the teeth" or "without breaking down," but should strive to be able to play *with* it, to toy with it, in order to have it at one's beck and call in any variation of mood, so as to play it as it pleases the mind and not only the fingers. One should acquire sovereignty over it.

This sovereignty is technique. But — technique is not art. It is only a means to achieve art, a paver of the path toward

A FOREWORD

it. The danger of confounding technique with art itself is not inconsiderable, since it takes a long time to develop a trustworthy technique; and this prolonged association with one subject is apt to give it supremacy over all others in one's mind. To guard against this serious danger the student should, above all, never lose sight of the fact that music, as does any other art, springs from our innate craving for individual expression. As word-thought is transmitted from man to man by verbal language so are feelings, emotions, moods — crystallized into tone-thought — conveyed by music. The effects of music may, therefore, be ennobling and refining; but they can as easily be degrading and demoralizing. For the saints and sinners among music-makers are probably in the same proportion as among the followers of other professions. The ethical value of music depends, therefore, not upon the musician's technique, but solely upon his moral tendencies. The student should never strive to dazzle his auditor's ear with mere technical brilliancy, but should endeavour to gladden his heart, to refine his feelings and sensibilities, by transmitting noble musical thoughts to his mind. He should scorn all unnecessary, charlatanish externalities and strive ever for the inwardness of the composition he interprets; for, in being honest to the composition he will also be honest to himself and thus, consciously or not, express his own best self. If all musicians were sincere in this endeavour there could be neither envy nor jealousy among them; advancing hand in hand toward their common ideal they could not help being of mutual assistance to each other.

Art, not unlike religion, needs an altar around which its devotees may congregate. Liszt, in his day, had erected such an altar in Weimar, and as its high priest he stood, himself, before it — a luminous example of devotion to art. Rubinstein did the same in St. Petersburg. Out of these atmospheres, thanks to the inspiring influences of Liszt's and Rubinstein's wonderful personalities, there have emerged a large number of highly meritorious and some eminent artists. That many of them have lacked the power in their later life to withstand the temptations of quick material gain by descending to a lower plane is to be regretted, but — such is life. Many are called, but few are chosen. Since those days several of these "many" have attempted to create similar centres in Europe. They failed, because they were not serving art, but rather made art serve their own worldly purposes.

The artists of talent no longer group themselves around the man of genius. Perhaps he is not to be found just now. Each little celebrity among the pianists keeps nowadays a shop of his own and all to himself. Many of these shops are "mints," and some of them produce counterfeits. As a matter or course, this separative system precludes all unification of artistic principles and is, therefore, very harmful to the present generation of students. The honest student who will discriminate between these, sometimes cleverly masked, counterfeit mints, and a real art altar must be of a character in which high principles are natively ingrained. It might help him somewhat to remember that when there is no good to choose we can always reject the bad.

What is true of teachers is just as true of compositions. The student should not listen to — should not, at least, repeat the hearing of — bad compositions, though they may be called symphonies or operas. And he can, in a considerable measure, rely upon his own instincts in this matter. He may not — and probably will not — fully fathom the depths of a new symphony at its first hearing, but he must have received general impressions of sufficient power and clearness to make him *wish* for another hearing. When this wish is absent he should not hear the work again from a mere sense of duty; it were far wiser to avoid another hearing, for habit is a strong factor, and if we accustom our ear to hear cacophonous music we are apt to lose our aversion to it, which is tantamount to a loss of good, natural taste. It is with much of modern music as it is with opium, morphine, and other deadly drugs. We should shun their very touch. These musical opiates are sometimes manufactured by persons of considerable renown; of such quickly gained renown as may be acquired nowadays by the employment of commercialistic methods; a possibility for which the venal portion of the public press must bear part of the blame. The student

should not be deceived by names of which
the general familiarity is of too recent a
date. I repeat that he should rather consult his own feelings and by following them
contribute his modest share toward sending
some of the present "moderns" back into
their deserved obscurity and insignificance.

I use the term "moderns" advisedly,
for the true masters — some of whom
died but recently — have never stooped to
those methods of self-aggrandisement at
which I hinted. Their places of honour
were accorded to them by the world
because they were theirs, by right of their
artistic power, their genius and the purity
of their art. My advice to the students
and to all lovers of music is: Hold on with
all your might to the school of sincerity
and chastity in music! It is saner and,
morally and æsthetically, safer than the
entire pack of our present nerve-tickling,
aye, and nerve-racking "modernists."
Music should always elevate; it should
always call forth what, according to the
demands of time and place, is best in us.
When, instead of serving this divine mission,
it speculates upon, and arouses, our lowest
instincts for no better purpose than to fill

the pockets of its perpetrator, it should receive neither the help nor the encouraging attention of any noble-thinking and clean-minded man or woman. Passive resistance can do a good deal on these premises.

The matter of abstention from a certain type of music recalls to my mind another evil from which Americans should abstain; it is the curious and out-of-date superstition that music can be studied abroad better than here. While their number is not very large, I personally can name five American teachers who have struggled here for many a year without gaining that high recognition which they deserve. And now? Now they are in the various capitals of Europe, receiving the highest fees that were ever paid for instruction, and they receive these high fees from American students that throng their studios. That the indifference of their compatriots drove these men practically out of their country proved to be of advantage to them; but how ought those to be regarded who failed to keep them here? The wrong is irreparable in so far as these men do not think of returning to America except as visitors. The duty of American students and lovers of good music is to see to it that such capable teachers as *are* still here should *remain* here. The mass of emigration to Europe of our music students should cease! If a student has what is understood by "finished" his studies here and his teacher sets him free, he may make a reconnoitring tour in Europe. The change of views and customs will, no doubt, broaden his mind in certain directions. But musically speaking, he will be sure to find that most of the enchantment of Europe was due to its distance. Excepting the excellent orchestras of Europe and speaking of the general music-making there, it is at present not quite as good as it is here: neither is the average music teacher in Europe a whit better than the man of equal standing here.

Americans should take cognizance of the fact that their country has not stood still in music any more than in any other direction. Each year has recorded an advancing step in its development. We must cease to compare the Europe of to-day with the America of fifty years ago. At present there is an astonishingly large number of clever and capable musicians in America, and, as with good physicians and lawyers, their ability usually stands in inverse proportion to the amount of their advertising. It is these worthy teachers for whose sake the superstition of "studying abroad" should be foresworn. What Uncle Sam has, in the field of music, not directly produced he has acquired by the natural law of attraction; now that so many talented and learned instructors, both native and foreign, are here they should be given a fair opportunity to finish a pupil's development as far as a teacher can do it, instead of seeing him, half-done, rush off "to Europe." If I were not convinced that a change on this score is possible, I should not have devoted so many words to it. It is merely a question of making a start. Let me hope that each reader of this little book may start this change, or, that, if already started, he will foster and help it. If his efforts should be disparaged by some, he need not feel disheartened, but remember that he belongs to the "land of limitless possibilities."

JOSEF HOFMANN.

PIANO QUESTIONS

TECHNIQUE

1. GENERAL

What are the different techniques, and which one is most generally used? What is the difference between them?

What Does "Technique" Mean?

Technique is a generic term, comprising scales, arpeggios, chords, double notes, octaves, legato, and the various staccato touches as well as the dynamic shadings. They are all necessary to make up a complete technique.

Why do pianists who have more technique than many others practise more than these others?

The More Technique the More Practice

Why have the Rothschilds more secretaries than I have? Because the administration of a large fortune entails more work than that of a small one. A pianist's technique is the material portion of his artistic possessions; it is his capital. To keep a great technique in fine working trim is in itself a considerable and time-absorbing task.   And, besides, you know that the more we have the more we want. This trait is not only human; it is also pianistic.

How to Im-prove the Technique   Should I endeavour to improve my technique by trying difficult pieces?

You should not confine yourself to pieces that come easy to you, for that would prevent all further technical progress.   But beware of pieces that are so difficult that you could not play them — in a slower tempo — with absolute correctness.   For this would lead to the ruin of your technique and kill the joy in your studies.   Play pieces that are always a trifle harder than those you have completely mastered.   Do not emulate those who say: "I play already this or that," without asking themselves "how" they play. Artistry depends ever upon the "how."

2. POSITION OF THE BODY

Do Not Raise the Piano-Stool Too High   Are the best results at the piano attained by sitting high or low?

As a general rule, I do not recommend a high seat at the piano, because this induces the employment of the arm and shoulders rather than of the fingers, and is, of course, very harmful to the technique. As to the exact height of the seat, you will have to experiment for yourself and find out at which height you can play longest with the least fatigue.

Is my seat at the piano to be at the same height when I practise as when I play for people? *The Height of the Piano Seat*

Yes! Height and distance (from the keyboard) of your chair — which should never have arms — you should decide for yourself and once for all time; for only then can you acquire a normal hand position, which, in its turn, is a condition *sine qua non* for the development of your technique. See also to it that both feet are in touch with their respective pedals so as to be in place when their action is required. If they stray away and you must grope for the pedals when you need them it will lead to a break in your concentration, and this will cause you to play less well than you really can. To let the feet stray from the pedals easily affects your entire position. It is a bad habit. Alas, that bad habits are so much easier acquired than good ones!

3. POSITION OF THE HAND

The Tilt of The Hand in Playing Scales   Should my hand in playing scales be tilted toward the thumb or toward the little finger? I find that in the scales with black keys it is much easier to play the latter way.

I quite share your opinion, and extend it also to the scales without black keys. I think the natural tendency of the hands is to lean toward the little finger, and as soon as you have passed the stage of preliminary training, as soon as you feel fairly certain that your fingers act evenly, you may yield to their natural tendency, especially when you strive more for speed than force; for speed does not suffer tension, while force craves it.

4. POSITION OF THE FINGERS

The Results Count, Not the Methods   Does it make any difference if my fingers are held very much curved or only a little? I was told that Rubenstein used his fingers almost flat.

Since you mention Rubinstein I may quote his saying: "Play with your nose, if you will, but produce euphony (*Wohlklang*) and I will recognize you as a master of your instrument." It is ever a question of the result, whether you play this way or that way. If you should play with very much curved fingers and the result should sound uneven and pieced, change the curving little by little until you find out what degree of curvature suits your hand best. Experiment for yourself. Generally speaking, I recommend a free and easy position of hand and fingers, for it is only in a position of greatest freedom that their elasticity can be preserved, and elasticity is the chief point. By a free and easy position I mean that natural position of hand and fingers into which they fall when you drop your hand somewhat leisurely upon the keyboard.

Should a cantabile passage be played with a high finger-stroke or by using the weight of the arm? *Cantabile Passages*

Certain characteristic moments in some pieces require the high finger-stroke. It may be used also in working up a climax, in which case the raising of the fingers should increase proportionately to the rise of the climax. Where, however, the strength of the fingers is sufficient to obtain the climacteric result by pressure, instead of the stroke, it is always preferable to use pressure. As a general principle, I believe in the free-hanging, limp arm and recommend using its weight in cantabile playing.

An Incorrect Position of the Fingers
Pray how can I correct the fault of bending out the first joints of the fingers when their cushions are pressed down upon the keys?

Your trouble comes under the head of faulty touch, which nothing will correct but the constant supervision by a good teacher, assisted by a strong exertion of your own will power and strictest attention whenever you play. This bending out of the first joint is one of the hardest pianistic ailments to cure, but it is curable. Do not be discouraged if the cure is slow. The habit of years cannot be thrown off in a day.

5. ACTION OF THE WRIST

Should the hands be kept perfectly still in playing scales and arpeggios? Or, to lessen fatigue, is an occasional rise and fall of the wrist permissible in a long passage of scale or arpeggio? *Don't Stiffen the Hands in Playing Scales*

The hands should, indeed, be kept still, but not stiff. Protracted passages of scales or arpeggios easily induce a stiffening of the wrist. Hence, an occasional motion of the wrist, upward and downward, will do much to counteract this tendency. It will, besides, be a good test of the looseness of the wrist.

Is it not impossible to preserve a complete looseness of the wrist in piano-playing because of the muscles that connect the forearm with the hand? *The Loose Wrist*

By no means. You should only see to it that you do not stiffen the wrist *unconsciously*, as most players do. The arm should be held so that the wrist is on a line with it, not bent, and by concentrated thinking you should endeavour to transfer the display of force to the finger-tips instead of holding the tension in your arm. For this produces fatigue, while the way I suggest will lead you to develop considerable force through the hand and fingers alone and leave the arm practically limp and loose. It takes months of study under closest attention, however, to acquire this looseness of the arm.

The Position of the Wrist   Do you favour a low or high position of the wrist for average type of work?

For average work, I recommend an average position; neither high nor low. Changes, upward or downward, must be made to meet the requirements of special occasions.

Do Not Allow the Wrist to Get Stiff   If one's wrist is stiff is there any set of exercises especially adapted to acquiring a freer movement? Or is there any special method of exercise?

It depends on whether your wrist is stiff from non-use or from wrong use. Assuming the latter, I should recommend studies in wrist octaves, but you must watch your wrist while playing and rest at the slightest indication of its stiffening.

6. ACTION OF THE ARM

I cannot play tremolo in the left hand for any length of time without great fatigue. I have tried changing the position of the hand from high to low, the sidewise motion, and the quiet hand. What is the correct method, and may the difficulty be overcome by slow practice? *When Tremolo Proves Un duly Fatiguing*

The tremolo cannot be practised slowly, nor with a stiff or quiet hand. The action must be distributed over the hand, wrist, underarm and, if necessary, the elbow. The shoulder forms the pivot whence a vibratory motion must proceed and engage all the points on the road to the fingers. The division of labour cannot be done consciously, but should better proceed from a feeling as if the whole arm was subjected to an electric current while engaged in playing a tremolo.

Should octave chords be played with rigid arms, the wrists and fingers thereby increasing the tone volume, or should the arms be loose? My teachers differ in their methods; so I turn to you for advice. *Play Chords With a Loose Arm*

With few exceptions, dictated by certain characterizations, chords should always be played with a loose arm. Let the arm pull the hand above the keys and then let both fall heavily upon them, preparing the fingers for their appropriate notes while still in the air and not, as many do, after falling down. This mode of touch produces greater tone-volume, is least fatiguing, and will have no bad after-effects.

7. STRETCHING

Fatiguing the Hand by Stretching I stretch beween my fingers — taking the second and third, for instance, and trying to see how many keys I can get between them. It has helped me, but shall I be doing wrong to continue?

If, as you say, you feel benefited by your stretching exercises you may continue them. But in your place I should beware of fatigue, for while the hand may show an improvement in its stretch while you are practising these exercises, if it is fatigued it will afterward contract so that its stretch is liable to become narrower than it was before.

Is there any way to increase the stretch of my very small hand?

Any modern teacher, acquainted with your hand, can devise certain exercises that will be applicable to your particular hand. As the lack of stretch, however, may be due to a number of different causes I should advise you to desist from any stretch exercise that might be recommended to you without a close examination of your hand, since the wrong kind of exercise is not only apt, but bound, to injure it, perhaps permanently.

Is there any exercise, on the piano or otherwise, that would tend to stretch my hand so as to enable me to play octaves? My fingers are short and stubby. My teacher has not given me anything definite on this score.

The attempts to widen the natural stretch of the hand by artificial means lead easily to disastrous results. It was by just such attempts that Schumann rendered his hand useless for piano-playing. The best I can recommend is that before playing you soak your hands in rather hot water for several minutes and then — while still in the water — stretch the fingers of one hand with the other. By doing this daily you will gain in stretch, provided you refrain from forcing matters, and provided also that you are still young, and your hands are flexible.

8. THE THUMB

"What is the Matter With My Scales?" What is the matter with my scales? I cannot play them without a perceptible jerk when I use my thumb. How can I overcome the unevenness?

In answering this question I am in the position of a physician who is expected to prescribe a treatment for a patient whom he has neither examined nor even seen. I can therefore advise only in a very general way — as I have done with many questions to avoid the eventuality of being confronted by an exceptional case. The cause of the hand's unrest in the passing of the thumb lies usually in transferring the thumb too late. The thumb waits usually until the very moment when it is needed and then quickly jumps upon the proper key, instead of moving toward it as soon as the last key it touched can be released. This belatedness causes a jerky motion of the arm and imparts it to the hand. Another cause lies in a fault no less grave than the first. Since the hand has only five fingers while the scale numbers many notes (according to its length), the player must replenish his fingers by passing the thumb under the hand so as to form a conjunction between the notes played and those to be played. This passing of the thumb conditions a change or shifting of the hand toward the keys to follow, but the shifting of the hand must not coincide with the passing of the thumb or the result will be a jerk. The position of the hand in relation to the keyboard must not change. It must remain the same until the thumb has struck its new key. Not until then must the shifting of the hand take place. In this way the jumpiness or jerkiness of the scale can be avoided, provided one can follow this precept punctiliously — which is not an easy matter, espeeially in great speed. Alas, why are those pesky scales so difficult, in fact, the most difficult thing to do on the piano?

How to Hold the Thumb What is the correct position for the thumb? Should it be curved well under the hand while playing?

In scale-playing the thumb should be slightly curved and kept near the index finger in order to be ready when needed. In pieces this position of the thumb cannot, of course, always be observed.

Which Fingers Demand Most Attention? Should one pay special attention to the training of the thumb?

It may be said that the thumb and the middle finger are the two arch-conspirators against a precise finger technique. They crave your greatest attention. Above all, you must see to it that, in touching the keys with these fingers, you do not move the whole hand, still less the arm.

9. THE OTHER FINGERS

The Fourth and Fifth Fingers What exercise would you recommend for the training of the fourth and the fifth fingers?

Any collection of Etudes is sure to

contain some that are devoted to the training of those two fingers. In the Cramer Etudes (Bulow's selection) you will find Nos. 9, 10, 11, 14, 19, 20 adapted to your case, but do not pin your faith to the print! In all matters of art the "how" is of far more consequence than the "what." Play what you will, but bear your weak points in mind while you play. This is the real remedy. Keep hand and arm as loose as you can while training the fourth and fifth fingers.

In making wide skips in which the little finger strikes a single note, as, for instance, in left-hand waltz accompaniments, should one strike on the end of the little finger or on its side; and should the finger be curved or held more or less flat? *The Action of the Little Finger*

The little finger should never strike with its side. It should always be held in its normally curved condition, and straighten at the stroke only on such occasions when its own force proves insufficient and requires the assistance of the wrist and arm muscles.

10. WEAK FINGERS, ETC.

To Strengthen the Weak Finger   How can I strengthen the little finger of my right hand? I avoid it in playing, using the next finger instead.

Use It   By employing your little finger as much as possible and at once quitting the habit of substituting another finger for it.

The Weak Fingers of the Left Hand   What exercise would you recommend for the training of the fourth and fifth fingers of the left hand?

Slow trill with various touches, with highly lifted fingers producing strength through their fall and with a lesser lift of the fingers combined with pressure touch, watching closely that the little finger strikes with the tip and not with the side. Rhythmic evenness should also be punctiliously observed.

When the Fingers Seem Weak   What kind of technical work would you advise me to take to make my fingers strong in the shortest time consistent with good work?

If your fingers are unusually weak it may be assumed that your muscular constitution in general is not strong.

The training of the fingers alone will,
in that case, lead to no decisive results.
You will have to strive for a general
strengthening of your muscular fibre.
At this point, however, begins the
province of your physician and mine
ends. If you consider your constitution normal, four or five hours' daily
work at the piano will develop the
necessary digital force, if that time
is judiciously used.

Is it always necessary to watch the *No Ne-*
fingers with the eye? *cessity to*
In places where the fingers slide, and *Watch the*
do not jump from one note to another *Fingers*
at a distance, there is no need of keeping
the eye on them.

Is biting the finger-nails injurious to *Biting the*
the piano touch? *Finger-*
Certainly; biting the nails or any *Spoils the*
other injury to the finger-tips and hand *Touch*
will spoil your touch. Extreme cleanliness and care in cutting the nails
the proper length are necessary to keep
your hands in condition for playing
the piano.

To Prevent Sore Finger-Tips After Playing — How can I prevent my finger-tips, after prolonged playing, from feeling sore the next day?

Experience teaches that in such cases, as in many others, cleanliness is the best remedy. After playing wash your fingers at once in warm water, with soap and brush, and then rub them well with either cold cream or some similar fatty substance. In the development of speed on the piano, the rigidity of the skin on the fingers is a great hindrance; it makes us feel as if we played with gloves on the fingers.

Broad-Tipped Fingers Not a Disadvantage — Are broad-tipped fingers considered a detriment to a man student of piano; for instance, if the finger grazes the black keys on each side when playing between them?

Unless broad-tipped fingers are of an unusual thickness I do not consider them an obstacle in the way of good piano-playing; the less so, as the white keys — whatever shape the fingers may have — should never be struck between the black ones, but only in the midst of the open space. Altogether, I hold that the shape

of the hand is of far greater importance
to the pianist than the shape of his fingers;
for it furnishes the fingers with a base of
operations and with a source of strength,
besides holding the entire control over
them. Studying the hands and fingers
of celebrated pianists you will find a
great variety of finger shapes, while their
hands are usually broad and muscular.

When playing a piece in which a rest *What to do*
of a measure and a half or two measures *With the*
occurs should I drop my hand in my lap *Unemployed*
or keep it on the keyboard? *Hand*

If the temporarily unemployed hand
is tired it will rest better in the lap,
because this position favours the blood
circulation, which, in its turn, tends to
renew the strength. I should, however,
not put it away from the keyboard too
often, for this might easily be taken for
a mannerism.

11. STACCATO

What can I do to enable me to play *Wrist Stac-*
wrist staccato very fast without fatiguing *cato at a*
the arm? *High*
Tempo

Change your wrist staccato for a

little while to a finger or arm staccato, thus giving the wrist muscles a chance to rest and regain their strength.

*The Differ-
ence
Between
"Finger
Staccato"
and Other
Kinds*

What does "finger staccato" mean? Is not staccato always done with the fingers?

By no means! There is a well-defined arm staccato, a wrist staccato, and a finger staccato. The latter is produced by a touch similar to the rapid repetition touch — that is, by not allowing the fingers to fall perpendicularly upon the keys, but rather let them make a motion as if you were wiping a spot off the keys with the finger-tips, without the use of the arm, and rapidly pulling them toward the inner hand. The arm should take no part in it whatever.

12. LEGATO

*The Ad-
vantage of
Legato
Over
Staccato*

Is it better for me to practise more staccato or more legato?

Give the preference to legato, for it produces the genuine piano tone, and it develops the technique of the fingers; while the staccato touch always tends to draw the arm into action. If you play from the arm you cannot expect any benefit for the fingers. For the acquisition of a legitimate legato Chopin's works cannot be highly enough recommended, even in the transcriptions by Godowsky, which become impossible when tried with any touch other than legato. He wrote them, so to speak, out of his own hand, and his legato is so perfect that it may well be taken as a model by anybody.

Should you advise me to make use of a high finger-stroke? My teacher makes me use it exclusively, but I notice that my playing is neither legato nor quiet. It is almost humpy. *To Produce Good Legato*

Your manner of putting the question expressed your own — and correct — judgment in the matter. This playing "in the air" is lost energy, and will not lead to a good legato. The most beautiful tone in legato style is ever produced by a "clinging and singing" gliding of the fingers over the keys. Of course, you have to watch your touch in order that your "clinging" does not deteriorate into "blurring," and that your "gliding" may not turn into "smearing." If you apprehend any such calamity you must for a while increase the raising of your fingers and use more force in their falling upon the keys. Under constant self-observation and keen listening you may, after a while, return to the gliding manner. This much in general; of course, there are places and passages where just the opposite of my advice could be said, but still I think that the high finger-stroke should rather be employed for some special characteristic effects than as a general principle.

The Firm and Crisp Legato Touch I am confused by the terms "firm legato touch" and "crisp legato touch." Wherein lies the difference?

Legato means "bound together," for which we substitute the word "connected." Two tones are either connected or they are not connected. The idea of various kinds of legato is purely a sophism, a product of non-musical hyper-analysis. By "legato" I understand the connecting of tones with each other through the agency of the fingers (on the piano). The finger that evoked a tone should not

leave its key until the tone generated
by the next finger has been perceived
by the ear. This rule governs the playing
of melodies and slow passages. In rapid
passages, where the control through the
ear is lessened, the legato is produced
by more strictly mechanical means, but
there should, nevertheless, always be
two fingers simultaneously occupied. Do
not take the over-smart differentiations
of legato seriously. There is no plural
to the word "legato."

13. PRECISION

My teachers have always scolded me *Not Play-*
for playing my left hand a little before *ing the*
my right. It is probably a very bad *Two*
habit, but I do not hear it when I do it. *Hands at*
How can I cure it? *Once*

This "limping," as it is called, is the
worst habit you can have in piano playing,
and you are fortunate in having a teacher
who persists in his efforts to combat it.
There is only one way to rid yourself of
this habit, namely, by constant attention
and closest, keenest listening to your
own playing. You are probably mis-
stating it when you say that you do not

"hear" it when you "limp"; it seems
more likely to me that you do not listen.
Hearing is a purely physical function
which you cannot prevent while awake,
while listening is an act of your will-
power — it means to give direction to
your hearing.

14. PIANO TOUCH *vs.* ORGAN TOUCH

*How
Organ-
Playing
Affects the
Pianist*

Is alternate organ and piano playing
detrimental to the "pianistic touch"?

Inasmuch as the force of touch and its
various gradations are entirely irrelevant
on the organ, the pianist who plays much
on the organ is more than liable to lose
the delicacy of feeling for tone-production
through the fingers, and this must, naturally, lessen his power of expression.

*Organ-
Playing
and the
Piano
Touch*

Is it true that a child beginning music
lessons on an organ gets much better
tone than one beginning on a piano, and
does the side study of pipe-organ, after
two years of extensive piano work, impair
the piano touch?

It is only natural that a child can get
better tone out of an organ than on a
piano, because it is not the child but the

organ that produces the tone. If the child's purpose, however, is to learn piano-playing it would not be wise to let him begin on an organ, because this would leave the essential element — the art of touch — entirely undeveloped. And if his piano touch has been formed it can easily be undone again by letting him play on the organ.

15. FINGERING

In what respect does American finger-ing differ from foreign fingering, and which offers the greater advantages?

The Universal System of Marking Fingering

There is no "American" fingering. Many years ago the "English" fingering (which counts only four fingers and a thumb, and indicates the latter by a plus mark: +) was adopted by a few of the less prominent publishers in America; but it was soon abandoned. If you have a piece of sheet music with English fingering you may be certain that it is not of a recent edition, and I would advise you to obtain a more modern one. The advantage of the universal fingering lies in its greater simplicity, and in the circumstance that it is universally adopted.

The C-Scale Fingering for All Scales? Do you advise the use of the C-scale fingering for all the scales? Is it practicable?

The C-scale fingering is not applicable to scales reposing on black keys because it creates unnecessary difficulties, the mastering of which would be a matter rather of mere sport than of art.

Fingering the Chromatic Scale Which fingering of the chromatic scale is most conducive to speed and accuracy?

The right thumb always upon E and B, the left one upon F and C. Between times use three or four consecutive fingers as often as convenient. At the beginning of a long chromatic scale select such fingers as will most naturally bring you to one of the stations just mentioned.

The Fingers Needed to Play a Mordent When executing the mordent, is not the use of three fingers preferable to two?

The selection of the fingers for the execution of a mordent depends always upon the preceding notes or keys which lead up to it. Since we cannot lift the hand just before a mordent for the purpose of changing fingers (for this would mean a rude interruption) we have to use whatever fingers happen to be "on hand." An exchange of fingers in a mordent is seldom of any advantage, for it hampers precision and evenness, since, after all, each finger has its own tone-characteristics.

16. THE GLISSANDO

Will you describe the best method of holding the hand when playing glissando? Which is preferable to use, the thumb or the forefinger?

To Play a Glissando Passage

In playing glissando in the right hand use the index finger when going upward, the thumb when going downward. In the left hand — where it hardly ever occurs — use the middle finger in either direction, or, if you should find it easier, the index finger downward. The production of so great a volume of tone, as is possible on our modern piano, has necessitated a deeper fall of the keys than former pianos possessed, and this deeper dip has banished the glissando almost entirely from modern piano literature.

17. OCTAVES

Should I play octaves using the 'hinge" stroke from the wrist or by using the arm? I find I can get more

How Best to Play the Octaves

tone by using the arm stroke, but cannot play so rapidly.

The character of the octaves must govern the selection of means to produce them. For light octaves use the wrist, for heavier ones draw more upon the arm. Rapidity requires that you avoid fatigue. If you feel fatigue approaching from too constant use of one joint, change to the other, and in doing this change also the position of the hand from high to low, and *vice versa*. For wrist octaves I recommend the low position of the hand, for arm octaves the high one.

Rapid Octaves Please suggest some method of playing octaves rapidly to one who finds this the most difficult part of piano-playing. Would be grateful also for naming some octave études that could be used in the repertoire.

If rapid octaves seem to be "the most difficult part of piano-playing" to you, take it as an indication that they do not suit your nature. A "method" will never change your nature. This need not discourage you, however; it is only to prevent you from trying to make a specialty of something for which you are not especially qualified and to save you a needless disappointment. Hold arms and hands in but a slight tension, and at the slightest fatigue change the position of the hand from high to low and *vice versa*. Your seat at the piano should not be too low. Study the first book of Kullak's Octave School, and, later on, the second book.

When should I use the arm to play octaves as I have seen some concert players do? As I was watching them there did not seem to be the slightest motion from the wrist. *When Playing Octaves*

Most concert players play their octaves more from the arm than from the wrist, but their wrist is nevertheless not so inactive as it seems to have appeared to you. They have probably distributed the work over the wrist, the elbow, and the shoulder in such a way that each had to do only a part of it. Light octaves can come only from the wrist, while heavier ones put the elbow and shoulder into action. To make this distribution consciously is hardly possible.   A striving for economy of force and the least possible fatigue will produce this "division of labour" unconsciously.

Wrist Stroke in Long Octave Passages   When playing extended octave passages, such as the Liszt arrangement of "The Erlking," should the endeavour be to play all from the pure wrist stroke; or is it well to relieve the strain by an occasional impulse (a sort of vibration) from the forearm? Is there any advantage in varying the height of the wrist?

In extended octave playing it is well to vary the position of the wrist, now high and then low. The low position brings the forearm into action, while the whole arm coöperates when the wrist is held high. From the wrist alone such pieces as "The Erlking" cannot be played, because the wrist alone gives us neither the power nor the speed that such pieces require. Besides, the octaves, when all played from the wrist, would sound "cottony." The wrist alone is to be used only in light, graceful places.

In playing octaves or other double *Stiff Wrists*
notes my wrist seems to stiffen. How *in Playing*
Octaves
can I remedy this?

Stiffness in the wrist results from an
unmindful use of it. When practising
octaves or double notes think always of
holding the arm and its joints in a loose,
limber condition, and when you feel fatigued do not fail to stop until the muscular contraction is relieved. In a little
while you will see your conscientious
practising rewarded by acquiring an
elasticity commensurate with your general
physical status.

Why does it tire my arms when I play *Premature*
octaves and a continuation of little runs? *Fatigue*
in the
How can I avoid it, so that they will feel *Arms*
free and easy?

Premature fatigue is usually caused by
undue muscular contraction. Keep your
arms and wrists loose and you will find
that the fatigue disappears. For your
sensation of fatigue may be due, not to
exhaustion of muscular power, but to
a stoppage of circulation caused by an
unconscious stiffening of the wrist.
Change the position of the wrist from

high to low and *vice versa* whenever you feel the "fatigue" coming on.

Kullak's Method of Octaves" Still Good Is Kullak's "Method of Octaves" still one of the best in its line? or can you recommend something better?

Since the days when Kullak's "School of Octaves" was printed, experience has taught us some things which might be added to it, but nothing that would contradict it. Nor, so far as I know, has anything better appeared in print than the first volume of that work especially.

18. REPETITION TECHNIQUE

The Diffi-culty of Playing Repetition Notes Please help me about my repetition notes. When I wish to play them rapidly it seems that the key does not always produce a sound? Is it because of my touch?

First, examine the action of your piano. It occurs not infrequently that the fingers do their work well, but fail in the results because of an inert or lazy piano action. If, however, the fault does not lie in the instrument, it must lie in a certain stiffness of the fingers. To eliminate this you need, first of all, a loose wrist. Furthermore, you should not, in repetition technique, let the fingers fall perpendicularly upon the keys, but with a motion as if you were wiping the keys with the finger-tips and then pull them quickly toward the palm of the hand, bending every joint of them rapidly.

19. DOUBLE NOTES

Please tell me something about the general practice of thirds, both diatonic and chromatic; also, about those in the first movement of the Grieg Concerto.

The Playing of Double Thirds

As the playing of passages in single notes requires a close single legato, to do double thirds requires an equally close double legato. As to the exact details of legato playing I may refer you to my book, "Piano Playing," where you will find the matter discussed at length in the chapter on "Touch and Technic."

THE INSTRUMENT

Is it irrelevant whether I practise upon a good or a bad piano?

The Kind of Piano Upon Which to Practise

For practice you should never use any but the very best available instrument.

Far, rather, may the piano be bad when you play for people. This will not hurt you nearly so much as will the constant and habitual use of a piano with a mechanism in which every key demands a different kind of touch, and which is possibly out of tune. Such conditions impair the development of your musical ear as well as of your fingers. It cannot be otherwise. As I said once before, learning means the acquiring of habits: habits of thinking and of doing. With a bad instrument you cannot develop any good qualities, even if you should possess them by nature; much less can you acquire them. Hence, I recommend a good piano, clean keyboard — for your æsthetic perceptions should be developed all around — a correct seat and concentration of mind. But these recommendations presuppose on the part of the student some talent and a good teacher.

Do Not Use a Piano Extreme in "Action"   Is it not better for a student in the advanced stage of study, who is preparing for concert work, to practise on a piano with a heavy action in order to develop the finger and hand muscles, and to use an instrument with a light action for obtaining an artistic finish to the lighter passages occurring so often, for instance, in Chopin's music?

All extremes are harmful in their effects upon study and practice. A too heavy action stiffens and overtires the fingers, while too light an action tends to impair your control. Try to obtain for your practice a piano the action of which approximates as nearly as possible that of the piano on which you have to play in the concert, in order to avoid unpleasant surprises, such as premature fatigue or a running away of the fingers.

Should I keep the action of my piano tight? *How Tight to Keep the Piano's Action*

Keep it tight enough to preserve the "feeling" of the keys under the fingers, but to make it more so would endanger your finger action and it may injure your hand.

Do you think it wise for a beginner to practise on a piano that has a heavy action? *The Action of a Beginner's Piano*

That depends upon the age and physical development of the beginner. "Heavy" and "light" action are not absolute but relative terms, which comprise in their meaning the power of resistance in the player's hand. The action should be so adjusted that the player can — even in the softest touch — always feel the key under his finger. A too heavy action leads necessarily to an employment of the shoulder muscles (which should be reserved for brief, special uses) and may permanently injure the hand.

Playing On a Dumb Piano   Are mechanical appliances, such as a dumb keyboard, of advantage to the student of the piano? Should its use be restricted to a particular stage in the course of study?

Music is a language. Schumann said: "From the dumb we cannot learn to talk!" The totally dumb or mute piano should, therefore, not be used, or very little, if we aim at a "musical" technique — that is, a live, multicoloured technique qualified to express musical thought and feeling.

Personally I have never used a dumb piano.

THE PEDALS

Should I use the pedal with each melody note? Should like a general rule. *A General Rule About the Pedal*

The treading upon the pedal should always follow immediately after the striking of the note for which it is intended, or else there will be discords arising from the mingling of that note with the one preceding it. This is the general rule. Exceptions there are, of course, but they occur only in certain moments when a mingling of tones is purposed for some special effect.

What is the use of the damper pedal? Primarily it serves to prolong such tones as we cannot hold with the fingers. But it is also one of the greatest means for colouring. The employment of it should always be governed by the ear. *The Use of the Pedal for Colouring*

Please tell me how to use the pedal. I find that in some pieces there is no mark under the measures to show me when it should be used. Is there any rule which you can give me? *How to Use the Pedal*

Assuming that you have in mind the artistic use of the pedal, I regret to say that there is no more a rule for this than for the mixing of colours upon the palette of a painter who strives for some particular shade or tint. He knows that blue and yellow make green, that red and blue make purple; but those are ground colours which he can rarely use. For the finer shades he has to experiment, to consult his eye and his judgment. The relation between the pedal and the player's ear is exactly similar to that of the palette and the painter's eye. Generally speaking (from sad experience) it is far more important to know when *not* to use the pedal than when to use it. We must refrain from its use whenever there is the slightest danger of unintentional mingling of tones. This is best avoided by taking the pedal *after* striking the tone upon which it is to act, and to release it promptly and simultaneously with the striking of the next tone. It may be at once taken again, and this alternation must be kept up where there is either a change of harmony or a succession of "passing notes." This is the only positive rule I can give, but even this is often violated. Let your ear be the guardian of your right foot. Accustom your ear to harmonic and melodic clarity, and — listen closely. To teach the use of the pedal independent of the action of your own ear is impossible.

In Weber's "Storm" should the pedal be held down throughout the entire piece, as directed? It produces quite a discord.

Let Your Ear Guide Your Pedalling

Without knowing this piece, even by name, I may say that the pianos of Weber's time had a tone of such short duration and volume that the discords resulting from a continuous use of the pedal were not so noticeable, as they are now upon the modern piano with its magnificent volume and duration of tone. Hence, the pedal must now be used with the utmost caution. Generally speaking, I say — again — that the ear is the "sole" guide of the foot upon the pedal.

Is Bach's music ever played with the pedal?

Use Pedal With Caution in Playing Bach

There is no piano-music that forbids the use of the pedal. Even where the texture of a piece does not require the pedal — which happens very rarely — the player might employ it as an aid where the reach of his hand proves insufficient to hold all the parts of a harmony together. With Bach the pedal is often very important; for, by judicious use — as, for instance, in the cases of organ-point — it accumulates harmonic tones, holds the fundamental tone and thus produces effects not dissimilar to the organ. Qualitatively speaking, the pedal is as necessary in Bach's music as in any other; quantitatively, I recommend the utmost caution in its use, so as not to blur the fine texture of his polyphony.

The Student with a Fondness for the Pedal I always want to use the pedal as soon as I take a new piece, but my teacher insists that I should get a good singing tone first. Is she right?

You "want" to use the pedal? In the face of your teacher's advice to the contrary? Then why did you apply for a teacher? People who consider their own pleasure while engaged in any kind of study need no teacher. They need discipline. Learn obedience! If

by following your teacher's advice you
should fail to progress, even then you
have no right to do anything else than
go to another teacher.   But he will in
all probability not be very different
from the first one in his precepts.   Hence,
I say again: You should learn obedience!

May the damper pedal and the soft *Using the*
pedal be used simultaneously, or would *Two Pedals*
this be detrimental to the piano? *at Once*

Since the mechanisms of the two pedals
are entirely separate and independent of
each other you may use them simultaneously, provided that the character of
a particular place in your piece justifies it.

Should the expresson "*p*" be executed *To Pro-*
by the aid of the soft pedal or through *duce a*
the fingers? *Softer*
Tone

The soft pedal serves to change the
quality of tone, not the quantity.   It
should therefore never be used to hide
a faulty *piano* (or soft) touch.   Mere
softness of tone should always be produced by a decrease of finger-force and a
lessening of the raising of the fingers.
The soft pedal should be employed only

when the softness of tone is coupled
with a change of colouring, such as lies
within its range of action.

*Do Not
Over-Use
the Soft
Pedal*
Should the Gavotte in A, of Gluck-
Brahms, be played without the soft pedal?
Does a liberal use of the soft pedal tend
to make the student lazy in using a light
touch?

Your first question is too general, as
there is no piece of music that should be
played entirely with or without the soft
pedal; it is used only when a certain
change of colouring is proposed. A too
frequent use of the soft pedal does tend
to a neglect of the *pianissimo* touch,
and it should, therefore, be discouraged.

*Once More
the "Soft"
Pedal*
My piano has a rather loud tone to
which my people object, and urge me to
play with the soft pedal. I use it most
of the time, but am afraid now to play
without it. What would you advise?

If a soft touch and sound are liked,
have the mechanism of your piano
changed at the factory. I found myself
in the bad condition at one time that I
could not play certain passages inde-
pendently of the position of my foot on

the soft pedal. Such is the strength of
association that very soon a constant use
of the soft pedal produces physical in-
ability to play unless the foot is pressing
the pedal.

PRACTICE

In resuming my studies in the morning *The*
what should I play first?   *Morning*
Begin with your technical work. Scales   *Practice*
in all tonalities, each at least twice well   *On the*
rendered. First slowly, one after an-   *Piano*
other, then somewhat quicker, but never
very quickly as long as you are not
absolutely sure that both hands are
perfectly even, and that neither false
notes nor wrong fingerings occur. To
play the scales wrong is just as much a
matter of habit as to play them right —
only easier. You can get very firmly
settled in the habit of striking a certain
note wrong every time it occurs unless
you take the trouble of counteracting
the formation of such a habit. After
these scales play them in octaves from
the wrist, slowly and without tiring it
by lifting the hand to a needless height.
After this play either Czerny or Cramer,

then Bach, and finally Mozart, Beethoven, Chopin, and so on. If you have the time to do it, play one hour in the morning on technical studies and use one hour for the difficult places in the works you are studying. In the afternoon play another hour, and this hour you devote to interpretation. I mean by this that you should now apply æsthetically what you have technically gained in the morning by uniting your mechanical advantages with the ideal conception which you have formed in your mind of the work you are studying.

Morning Is the Best Time to Practise How much time should I spend on clearly technical study ? I am practising three hours a day; how long should I practise at a time ?

Purely technical work — that is, work of the fingers without the participation of mind and heart — you should do little or none, for it kills your musical spirit. If, as you say, you practise three hours a day I should recommend two hours in succession in the morning and one hour in the afternoon. The morning is always the best time for work. Make no long pauses in your work, for they would break your contact with the piano and ti would take considerable time to reëstablish it. In the afternoon, after the major portion of your daily task is done, you may move with greater freedom, though even this freedom should be kept within proper bounds.

Should I practise studies in general for my progress or should I confine myself strictly to my technical exercises? *Time to Devote to Technical Exercises*

Your strictly technical exercises should occupy one-quarter of the entire time you can give to your work. Two quarters you should use for the technical preparation of the difficult passages you encounter in the pieces you are studying, and during the last quarter these passages which have been thus prepared should be ranged into their proper places in the pieces, in order that you may not lose your view of the totality of the pieces while studying or practising details.

In purely technical, *i. e.*, mechanical, practice may I have a book or a magazine on the music-stand and read? *The Only Kind of Practice Worth While*

This question will appear grotesque to

any one who has not thought of it, yet it is legitimate; for I know positively that this crime upon themselves has been committed by many. I cannot warn students too strongly against this pernicious habit. It is far better to practise only half as long, but with concentrated attention. Even purely mechanical matter must be transmitted to the motor-centres of the brain through the agencies of the ear and eye in order to bring beneficial technical results. If the brain is otherwise occupied it becomes insensible to the impression of the work in hand, and practise thus done is a complete waste of time. Not only should we not read, but also not think of anything else but the work before us, if we expect results. Concentration is the first letter in the alphabet of success.

Practising Eight Hours Instead of Four   Will I advance quicker by practising eight hours instead of four, as I do now?

Playing too much in one day has often a deteriorating effect upon one's studies, because work is profitable, after all, only if done with full mental concentra-

tion, which can be sustained only for a
certain length of time. Some exhaust
their power of concentration quicker
than others; but, however long it may
have lasted, once it is exhausted all
further work is like unrolling a scroll
which we have laboriously rolled up.
Practise self-examination, and if you
notice that your interest is waning —
stop. Remember that in studying the
matter of quantity is of moment only
when coupled with quality. Attention,
concentration, devotion, will make unnecessary any inquiries as to how much
you ought to practise.

Shall I, when my hands are cold and *Playing*
stiff, play at once difficult and fatiguing *With Cold*
things in order to limber them up? *Hands*
In forcing things with cold hands you.
always run the danger of overstraining,
while with a gradual limbering you may
safely try the same tasks with impunity.
Handle the piano lightly while the hands
are cold, and increase both force and
speed only when the hands have gained
their normal temperature and elasticity.
This may take half or even three-

quarters of an hour. It may be accelerated by putting the hands in hot water before playing, but this should not be done too often, because it is apt to weaken the nerves of the hands.

Counting Out Loud Is counting aloud injurious to a pupil's playing — that is, does not the sound of the voice confuse the pupil in getting the correct tone of the note struck?

Loud counting can hardly ever be injurious — especially not while the pupil is dealing with time and rhythm. This part mastered or fully understood, the audible counting may be lessened and finally abandoned. During practice loud counting is of inestimable value, for it develops and strengthens rhymthic feeling better than anything else will, and, besides, it is an infallible guide to find the points of stress in a phrase.

The Study of Scales Is very Important Must all study of the piano absolutely begin with the study of scales?

Scales should not be attempted until a good finger-touch has been formed and the very important action of the thumb in the scale has been fully prepared.

After that, however, I consider the practising of scales important, not only for the fingers, but also for the discipline of the ear with regard to the feeling of tonality (key), understanding of intervals, and the comprehension of the total compass of the piano.

Do you approve of the study of all the fifteen major scales by piano students, or is the practice of the enharmonic ones unnecessary? *The Study of the Scales*

One should learn everything in that line in order to select from one's store of learning that which the occasion calls for. Study or practise all scales as they are written, and later also in thirds, sixths, and octaves.

When studying a new composition, which is preferable: to practise first with separate hands or together? *When Reading Over a New Piece*

When first looking over a new composition both hands should be employed, if possible, for this is necessary to obtain, approximately, at least, a mental picture of it. If the player's technique is too insufficient for this the deciphering must, of course, be done for each hand separately.

Practising the Two Parts Separately   When I am learning a new piece should the hands practise their parts separately?

Provided you have formed a general idea of the piece, it is well to practise the hands separately, because you can, in this way, concentrate your attention upon the work of each hand. As soon, however, as each hand knows its work the hands should play together in order now to pursue the musical purpose for which the separate practice was only a technical preparation.

Four Ways to Study a Piano Piece   Should a composition be studied away from the piano?

There are four ways to study a composition:

1. On the piano with the music.
2. Away from the piano with the music.
3. On the piano without the music.
4. Away from the piano without the music.

2 and 4 are mentally the most taxing and fatiguing ways, no doubt; but they

also serve best to develop the memory and what we mean by "scope," which is a faculty of great importance.

How fast or slow should Schubert-Liszt's "*Auf dem Wasser zu singen*" be played? What modern parlour pieces would you recommend after Bendel's "Zephyr"? *The Conditions Which Dictate Speed in Playing*

Even if I did believe in metronomes, as I do not, I could not indicate speed for you or for anybody, because it will always depend upon the state of your technique and the quality of your tone. For modern parlour pieces I suggest the two volumes of Russian piano music published by G. Schirmer, New York. You will find pieces of various degrees of difficulty there from which you may select what suits you best.

Which is the best way to work up a fast tempo? *To Work Up a Fast Tempo*

The best help is to hear the piece or part which you have in mind played quickly by another person, for this aids you in forming the mental concept of it, which is the principal condition to which all ability is subject. There are, however, other ways which each one of us must find for himself: either by a gradual increase of speed until you reach your individual maximum or by starting at once at full tilt, even though some notes should drop under the piano and then be picked up in subsequent repetitions. Which of these two or any other ways is best for you no one can tell; your musical instinct will guide you if you follow it cautiously.

The Best Way to Work Up a Quick Tempo Is it ever a waste of time to practise a piece over and over again for months as slowly as a beginner and with utmost concentration? After having done so and gradually working up a tempo, I then find I cannot play so fast as I want to. Is it not wise to begin all over again as slowly as possible? I prefer to work this way, but have been told that one gets "stale," studying the same music for a long time.

Do you advise practising with or without the pedal?

Slow practice is undoubtedly the basis for quick playing; but quick playing is not an immediate result of slow practice. Quick playing must be tried from time to time, with increasing frequency and heightened speed, even at a temporary loss of clearness. This loss is easily regained by subsequent returns to slow practice. After all, we must first learn to think quickly through the course of a piece before we can play it quickly, and this mental endeavour, too, will be greatly aided by occasional trials in a quicker tempo. As for getting "stale," a variety of pieces is necessary to preserve the freshness of each one.

Regarding the pedal, I suggest that you use it judiciously from the very beginning of the study of a new piece; though never in finger exercises.

What is the purpose of associating *Watch* breathing with piano playing, and to *Your Breathing* what extent should it be practised?

Breathing is as important in piano playing as in all physical exertion, and more so when we speak of pieces that entail the use of great muscular force; for this causes a quickening in the action of the heart; respiration naturally keeps step with it, and the result is often a forcible breathing through the mouth. Players resort to open-mouth breathing in such cases because they cannot help themselves. If, at the last spurt of a bicycle race, we should call to the wheelmen, "Breathe through the nose!" we could not wonder if our advice remains unheeded. This open-mouth breathing, however, need not be learned; it is the self-help of nature. I recommend breathing through the nose as long as possible. It is more wholesome than mouth-breathing, and it refreshes the head more. When physical exertion becomes too great then you will neither need nor heed my advice or anybody's; your nature will find its own line of least resistance.

Take a Month's Rest Every Year

Must I keep up my practice during my Christmas holidays of a month?

If you have worked well on your development during the spring, summer, and autumn it will be to your advantage to stop your practising entirely for a month. Such a pause renews your forces as well as the love for your work, and you will, upon resuming it, not only catch up quickly with what you may think to have missed, but you will also make a quick leap forward because the quality of your work will be better than it could be if you had persisted in it with a fatigued mind. In a tired condition of mind and body we are very apt not to notice the formation of bad habits, and since "to learn means to form correct habits of thinking and doing" we must beware of anything that might impair our watchfulness as to bad habits. The greatest persistence cannot turn a bad habit into a virtue.

MARKS AND NOMENCLATURE

What is the meaning of M. M. = 72 printed over a piece of music?

The Metronome Markings

The M stands for "metronome," the other for the name of its inventor, Maelzl. The figures indicate the number of beats a minute and the note shows what each beat represents — in this case a quarter note. The whole annotation says that the average speed of the piece should admit of seventy-two quarter notes being played in a minute. I advise you, however, rather to consult the state of your technique and your own feeling for what is musically right in deciding upon the speed of the piece.

The Personal Element and the Metronome

In Chopin's Prelude No. 15 is the movement in C-sharp minor to be played in the same tempo as the opening movements, or much faster? How should the 6-8 and 9-8 movements of Liszt's Dance of the Gnomes be metronomized?

The C-sharp minor movement should not increase in speed, or only very little, because it rises to a considerable height dynamically, and this seems to counteract an increase of speed. As to the metronoming, I would not bother about it. The possibilities of your technique must ever regulate the speed question in a large degree. Tempo is so intimately related with touch and dynamics that it is in a large measure an individual matter. This does not mean that one may play andante where an allegro is prescribed, but that one person's allegro differs slightly from that of another person. Touch, tone, and conception influence the tempo. The metronome indications are to be accepted only with the utmost caution.

How fast, by metronome, should the minuetto of Beethoven's Sonatina, opus 49, Number 2, be played? *Metronome Markings May Better Be Ignored*

If you possess an edition of Beethoven that has no metronome marks you have been singularly fortunate, and I would not for the world interfere with such rare good luck. Consult your technique, your feelings, and have confidence in your good sense.

How should one use the metronome for practising? I have been warned against it, as my teacher tells me one is liable to become very stiff and mechanical by the persistent use of it. *There are Dangers in Using a Metronome*

Your teacher is eminently right. You should not play with the metronome for any length of time, for it lames the musical pulse and kills the vital expression in your playing. The metronome may well be used as a controlling device first, to find the approximate average speed of a piece, and, second, to convince yourself that, after playing for a while without it, your feelings have not caused you to drift too far away from the average tempo.

The Real Meaning of Speed Terms What is the meaning of the words Adagio, Andante, and Allegro? Are they just indications of speed?

They serve as such; though our musical ancestors probably selected these terms because of their indefiniteness, which leaves a certain margin to our individuality. Literally, Adagio (*ad agio*) means "at leisure." Andante means "going" in contradistinction to "running," going apace, also walking. Allegro (a contraction of *al leg-gie-ro*) means with "lightness, cheerful." Primarily these terms are, as you see, indications of mood; but they have come to be regarded as speed annotations.

A Rule For Selecting the Speed As the words "largo," "allegro," etc., are supposed to indicate a certain rate of speed, can you give a rule so that a student who cannot have the aid of a teacher will be able to understand in what time he should play a composition?

If the metronome is not indicated you

have to consult your own good taste.
Take the most rapid notes of your piece,
play them rapidly as the general trend
of the piece will æsthetically permit,
and adjust the general tempo accordingly.

How are the grace notes played in *How*
these measures from Chopin's Valse, *Grace*
Notes
opus 42, and when are grace notes not *Are*
struck simultaneously with the base? *Played*

Grace notes and their chiefs — that is,
those notes to which the grace notes are
attached — should ever be played with
one and the same muscular impulse.
The time occupied by the grace notes
should be so minimal that it should not
be discernible whether they appear simultaneously with the base note or slightly
before it.   In modern music it is usually
meant to precede the bass note, though
the good taste of the player may occasionally prefer it otherwise.

Rests Used Under or Over Notes   What is the meaning of a rest above or below the notes of the treble clef?

The rests you speak of can occur only when more than one voice (or part) is written in the same staff, and they indicate how long the entrance of the other voice is to be delayed.

What a Double Dot Means   What does it mean when a note is double-dotted, like ♪‥   I thought first it was a misprint, but it seems to occur too frequently for that.

As the first dot prolongs the note by one-half of its own value, so does the second dot add one-half of the value of the first dot.   A half-note with one dot lasts three-quarters, with two dots it lasts seven-eighths.

Should I accent the first note under a slur thus ♪   or should I lift my hand at the end of the slur thus ,

The Playing of Slurred Notes   Slurs and accents have nothing to do with each other, because accents relate to rhythm, while slurs concern the touch. The last note under a slur will usually be slightly curtailed in order to create that small pause which separates one phrase from another. Generally speaking, the slur in piano music represents the breathing periods of the vocalist.

What difference is there between a slur and a tie?

How a Tie and a Slur Differ

None in appearance, but much in effect. A tie continues the sound of the note struck at its beginning as long as the note-value at its end indicates. It can be placed only upon two notes of similar name in the same octave which follow each other. As soon as another note intervenes the tie becomes a slur and indicates a *legato* touch.

How should the beginning of slurs be accented?

Slurs and Accents Not Related

Slurs and accents have nothing to do with each other. Slurs indicate either a legato touch or the grouping of the notes. Which one of the notes thus grouped is to be accented depends upon its rhythmical position in the measure. The strong and weak beat (or positive and negative beat) govern the accent always, unless there is an annotation to the contrary, and such an annotation must be carried out with great judiciousness, seldom literally.

How Long an Accidental Affects a Note Where there is an accidental on the last beat of a measure does not that note resume its signature beyond the bar unless tied? The case I speak of was in a key of two flats, common time. The fourth beat, E, was naturalized and the first note of the next measure was E with the flat sign. I maintain that the flat sign is superfluous, and I should like to know if this is right?

You are quite right, theoretically. Nevertheless, the proper tonality signature of a note that was changed is very frequently restated when the same note recurs beyond the bar. Though this special marking is not necessary theoretically, practical experience has shown that it is not an unwise precaution.

"E-Sharp and B-Sharp" and the Double Flat What is the meaning of the sharps on the E and B line, and of a double-flat? Are they merely theoretical?

They are not theoretical, but orthographical. You confound the note C with the key on the keyboard by that name. B-sharp is played upon the key called C, but its musical bearing is very remote from the note C. The same applies to double-flats (and double-sharps), for D with a double-flat is played upon the key called C, but it has no relation to the note C. This corresponds precisely with the homonym in language: "sow" — "sew" — "so" — sound alike, but are spelled in various ways according to the meaning they are to convey.

How is an octave, written thus, to be played?

The Effect of Double Flats

As the single-flat lowers a note by a half-tone, so a double-flat lowers it by two half-tones or a full tone.

In playing an operetta recently I found the double-sharp sign (×) used for double-flats as well. Is this correct?

Double Sharp Misprinted for Double Flat

The sign may be a misprint. But if it should occur repeatedly I advise you to make quite sure, before taking the misprint for granted, that the sign is not, after all, meant for a double-sharp.

When an Accidental Is in Parentheses Please tell me how a chord or an interval marked thus ⎰ is executed. What does an acci- dental in parentheses mean?

Chords marked as above are slightly rolled in the same manner as if marked by a serpentine line, unless the sign denotes a linking with the other hand. Which of the two meanings is intended you will easily infer from the context. Accidentals in parentheses are mere warnings given by some composers wherever there is a possibility of doubt as to the correct reading caused by a momentary harmonic ambiguity. I have found these accidentals in parentheses so far only in the works of French composers.

The Staffs Are Independent of Each Other Does an accidental in the right hand influence the left?

Inasmuch as piano music is written in score form, the two staffs are as independent of each other as are the staffs in an orchestral score. We may, in cases of suspected misprints, draw certain inferences from one staff to the other, provided that they are justified by the prevailing harmony. As a rule, the two staffs are independent of each other in regard to accidental chromatic signs.

I am often asked why there must be *Why Two* fifteen keys in music instead of twelve— *Names* that is, why not always write in B instead *for the* of C-flat, in F-sharp instead of G-flat, in *"Same"* D-flat instead of C-sharp, or *vice versa?* *Key?* I can only say that the circle of fifths would not be complete without the seven scales in sharps and the seven in flats: but Bach does not use all the fifteen keys in his Forty-eight Preludes and Fugues, omitting entirely, in the major keys, G-flat, D-flat, and C-flat, and, in the minor keys, A-sharp and A-flat. Are compositions in sharps considered more brilliant than those in flats? Do composers consider modulation in selecting their key?

The answer to your question hinges upon whether you recognize in music mere tone-play or whether you concede a mental and psychic side to it. In the former case the mode of spelling a tone C-sharp or D-flat would be, indeed, irrelevant. But in the latter case you must admit the necessity of a musical orthography qualified to convey distinct tonal meanings and musical thoughts to the reader and to the player. Though there is in the tempered scale no difference between C-sharp and D-flat, the musical reader will conceive them as different from one another, partly because of their connection with other related harmonies. These determine usually the composer's selection in cases of enharmonic identities. In the script of human language you will find an analogy than which none could be more perfect. In English there are, for instance, "to," "too," and "two"; words in which the spelling alone, and not the sound of pronunciation, conveys the different meanings of the words.

The Meaning and Use of "Motif"   What is the meaning of a "motif"? What does a dash mean over a note? What is the best book of instruction for a beginner, a child of ten?

A motif is the germ of a theme. A theme may be composed of reiterations of a motif, or by grouping several motifs together; it may also combine both modes of procedure. The most glorious exemplification of construction by re-iteration of a motif you will find in the opening theme of Beethoven's Fifth Symphony. A dash over a note enjoins the player to hold that note with the finger until it has received its full value. The best "instruction book" for a child is a good teacher who uses no instruction book, but imparts his knowledge to the child from out of his own inner consciousness.

In playing notes written thus is it permissible to slide the fingers from the keys or should there be only a clinging touch?

Tied Stac-cato Notes

Notes marked as above are to be played in such a manner that each note is slightly separated from the next. The best touch for this is from the arm, so that the fingers are not lifted from their joints, nor from the wrist, but that the arm pulls the finger upward from the key.

What do short lines below or above a note or chord mean in contradistinction to a staccato or an accent? And does it affect the whole chord?

The "Tenuto" Dash and Its Effect

The dash under or above a note is a substitute for the word "tenuto" (usually abbreviated into "ten."), which means "held," or, in other words, be particular about giving this note its full sound-duration. This substitute is usually employed when the holding concerns a single note or a single chord.

A Rolled Chord Marked "Secco" How should I execute a chord that is written with a spread and also marked "secco"? — as in Chaminade's "Air de Ballet, No. 1."

Roll the chord as evenly as possible in all its parts; but use no pedal and do not hold it, but play it briskly and short.

Small Notes Under Large Ones What is the meaning of small notes printed under large ones?

Usually the small notes are an indication that they may be omitted by players who have not the stretch of hand necessary to play them.

Accenting a Mordent in a Sonata How should one play and accent the mordent occurring in the forty-seventh measure of the first movement — allegro di molto — of Beethoven's Sonata Pathétique, Opus 13?

The accent ought to lie upon the first note of the mordent, but you should not make a triplet of it by occupying the whole quarter with its execution. The mordent must be played fast enough to preserve the rhythmic integrity of the melody-note.

The Position of the Turn Over a Note

The turn ∾ stands sometimes directly over the note and sometimes farther to the right of it. Does this difference indicate different executions and, if so, how would the two turns have to be played?

The turn always begins with its uppermost note. When it stands directly over a note it takes the place of this note; when more to the right the note is struck first and the turn, judiciously distributed at the time of its disposal, follows.

How Are Syncopated Notes to be Played?

How are syncopated notes to be played?

Notes occurring an entire beat of the prescribed time are, when syncopated, to be played between the beats. If the syncopated notes occupy only a fraction of the beats they are played between the fractional beats.

A Trill Begins on the Melodic Note   In modern compositions should all trills begin upon the note which is written, presuming there is no appoggiatura before the note? Is the alternation of the thumb and the second finger desirable in the playing of a trill?

Where not expressly otherwise stated (by appoggiatura) trills usually begin upon the melodic tone (the note which is written). Change fingers when those employed get tired. For extended trills the use of three fingers is advantageous, while in shorter trills two fingers will preserve more clarity.

Position of Auxiliary Note in a Trill   In the accompanying example of the trill should the auxiliary note be a tone or a half-tone above the principal note? If the half-tone, what would be the name of the auxiliary note?

The episode you quote moves evidently in the tonality of G minor. The trill stands on B-flat. As the auxiliary note of a trill is ever the diatonic sequel of a stated note it must, in this case, be a whole tone above B-flat, namely C. Since the piece is written in D major there should have been a "natural" marked under the sign of the trill.

Will you kindly suggest a good method of gaining speed and smoothness in trilling ? *Speed and Smoothness in Trilling*
While there are no "methods" for trilling there are certain means by which sluggish muscles may be assisted. Yet, even these means cannot be suggested without knowing the seat and cause of your trouble. The causes differ with the individual, but they are, in the majority of cases, purely mental, not manual. To trill quickly we must think quickly; for if we trill only with the fingers they will soon stick, lose their rhythmic succession, and finish in a cramped condition. Hence, there is no direct way to learn trilling; it will develop with your general mental-musical advancement. The main thing is, of course,

always to listen to your own playing,
actually and physically, to perceive every
tone you play; for only then can you
form an estimate as to how quickly you
can "hear." And, of course, you do
not expect to play anything more quickly
than your own ear can follow.

Difference in Playing Trills What is the difference in the manner
of playing the trill in measure 25, and
those in measures 37 and 38, of the
Chopin Polonaise, Opus 53?

The significance of the trill in measure
25 is melodic, while that of the trills in
measures 37 and 38 is purely rhythmic,
somewhat in the nature of a snare-drum
effect. The first trill requires greater
stress on the melodic note, while in
the other two you may throw your
hand, so to speak, on both notes and
roll the trill until it lands upon the
next eighth-note.

The Meaning of Sol-feggio What is meant by "spelling" in music?
Unless it means the variety of ways
in which most chords can be written it
refers to an oral reciting of notes, properly
called solfeggio.

ABOUT CERTAIN PIECES AND COMPOSERS

Please tell me some pieces of the *Some* classics which are not too difficult for *Pieces for* my daughter of fourteen to play. She *a Girl of* has a great deal of talent but not much *Fourteen* technique. The Kuhlau Sonatinas she can play very well.

If your daughter is fourteen years old and has — as you say — much talent but little technique, it is high time to think of developing her technique, for a pianist without technique is like a pleasure traveller without money. At any rate, I should prefer the easier sonatas by Haydn and Mozart to those of Kuhlau, because of their greater intrinsic merit. Any good teacher will assist you in selecting them to fit your daughter's case.

In playing sonatas my teacher tells *In Playing* me it is a great fault if I neglect to ob- *a Sonata* serve the repeat marks. I have heard it said by others that the repetition is not necessary, though it may be desirable. Will you please give me your opinion?

In a sonata it is of serious importance to repeat the first part (exposition) of the first movement in order that the two principal themes, as well as their tributaries, may well impress themselves upon the mind and memory of your auditor. For, unless this is accomplished, he cannot possibly understand and follow their development in the next part. That the exposition part is not the only one to be repeated you will find frequently indicated; for instance, in the last movement of the "Appassionata," where the repetition is needful, not for the reason stated before, but for the sake of formal balance or proportion. Generally speaking, I am in favour of following the composer's indications punctiliously, hence, also, his repeat marks, which serve æsthetic purposes that you will perhaps not understand until later, when the sonata has, in your hands, outgrown the stage of being learned.

A Point in Playing the "Moonlight Sonata" Should not the notes of the triplet figure in Beethoven's "Moonlight Sonata" be so blended into each other that you do not hear them in separate notes, but as a background, so to speak, for the notes in the melody?

The truth lies midway between two extremes. While the accompaniment should be sufficiently subdued to form, as you say, a harmonic background, it ought, nevertheless, not to be blended to such a degree as to obliterate entirely the undercurrent of a triplet motion. The accumulation of each chord should be produced through the pedal, not through an excessive legato touch.

Should Mendelssohn's "Spring Song" be played in slow or fast time? *Playing the "Spring Song" too Fast*
It is marked "Allegretto grazioso." The latter term (graceful, in English) precludes a too-quick movement.

This is the seventh measure of Chopin's Polonaise, Opus 26, No. 1. What is *What a Dot May Mean* the meaning of the dot placed after the D in the bass? Whenever this measure is repeated the dot occurs, or I should have thought it a misprint.

The left-hand notes follow each other
as eighth-notes. Their respective duration, however, is indicated by the upward stems and the dot. It is intended
here that a complete chord should be
built up by accumulation, as in illustration *a:*

and I would also hold the fifth eighth as
in illustration *b.*

Where the Accent Should be Placed   In playing Chopin's Impromptu in
A-flat, Opus 29, should the first or the
last note of the mordent receive the
accent? I have heard the mordent sound
like a triplet? Is this the correct accent?

The last note of the mordent should be
accented in this case.

A Disputed Chopin Reading   In Chopin's Nocturne in F-sharp,
after the *Doggio* Movement, when re-
turning to Tempo I, and counting five
measures, should the right hand in the
fifth measure play this melody?

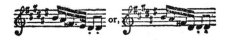

The various editions differ from one another in this measure. Peters's edition, generally considered the best edition of Chopin's works, has the second version, which commends itself by its greater naturalness.

In Rubinstein's "Melody in F" should the melody be played in the left hand or be divided between the two hands? *Playing the "Melody in F"*

Where there is no valid reason for doing otherwise it is always best to follow the composer's prescription; for, in most cases — and with great composers in all cases — the author knows what he meant to say. In the aforesaid piece, too, I advise you to adhere to this principle, since it is written with a view to teach the division of the melody-between the right and left hand. Any other execution would ruin this purposed design.

In Schumann's "Blumenstück," third number, the uppermost notes of the left hand are identical with the lowest of the right hand. Should the thumbs of both hands strike the same keys at the same *When Two Fingers Have the Same Note* time all the way through or should the left hand omit them?

The left hand should omit them, but be careful to omit only those that are really duplicates. There are a few places toward the end of each section where the left-hand notes differ from those in the right. In those cases you must be careful to play all the notes that are written.

BACH

The Be-ginner in Bach Music   Can you give me a few helpful suggestions in a preliminary study of Bach?

A totality consists of many parts. If you cannot master the totality of a work by Bach try each part by itself. Take one part of the right hand, one part of the left, add a third part, and so on until you have all the parts together. But be sure to follow out the line of each separate part (or "voice," as the Continentals say). Do not lose patience. Remember that Rome was not built in a day.

Bach's Music Necessary to Good Technique   Do you think the study of Bach is necessary to the development of one's technique, or should one let his music alone until a later day when one's technique is in good condition? Some of his music seems so dry.

Bach's music is not the only music that develops the technique. There is, for instance, the music of Czerny and Clementi to be considered. But Bach's music is particularly qualified to develop the fingers in conjunction with musical expression and thematic characterization. You may start with Czerny and Clementi, but you ought soon to turn to Bach. That some of his music seems dry to you may be due to your mental attitude by which you possibly expect from ecclesiastical music what only the opera can give you. Think yourself into his style and you will find a mine of never-dreamed-of enjoyment.

Do you think that the playing of Bach's works will keep one's hands in good technical condition? And which is the best edition of Bach's piano works? *Always Keep in Touch with Bach*

Bach is good for the soul as well as for the body, and I recommend that you never lose touch with him. Which is the best edition would be hard to

say, but I have found the Peters edition
to be very good.

Bach's   What is the plan of a "Fugue," how
Preludes does it differ from an "Invention"
and
Fugues   and "Prelude," and what is the purpose of studying the pieces so named
by Bach?

The explanation of the plan of a Fugue
would exceed by far the limits of the
space at my disposal. It would require
a text-book, of which there are many to
be found in every good music store. The
Fugue is the most legitimate representation of true polyphony. Its difference
from an Invention is expressed in the
two names. A Fugue (*fuga*, flight) is
the flight of one musical thought through
many voices or parts, subject to strict
rules, while an Invention is an accumulation of thoughts moving with absolute
freedom. The definition of Prelude, as
something which intentionally precedes
and fittingly introduces a main action,
fits the musical Prelude perfectly;
especially in the case of Bach. The
purpose of all these forms is that of
all good music-making, namely, the

purification and development of good taste in music.

Of the Bach fugues do you consider the C sharp major difficult to memorize, or do you advise the use of the D flat arrangement instead? *As to the Bach Fugues*

Such little differences have never bothered me, and I can therefore hardly answer your question definitely. It has been frequently observed — though never explained — that to many people it comes easier to read music in D flat than in C sharp. Hence, if you prefer the D flat edition it will reduce the difficulty for you. Possibly this more accessible version may aid you optically or visually in your work of memorizing.

BEETHOVEN

I am just beginning to reach an intelligent interpretation of Beethoven's music. Now, in what order should the Sonatas be studied? *Order of Studying Beethoven's Sonatas*

If you should really have the laudable intention to study all the Sonatas of Beethoven for your repertory I should think that you may safely take them up very much in the order in which they are printed, with the exception of Opus 53 and the Appassionata, which — spiritually as well as technically — rank with the last five. The Steingräber edition, however, furnishes a very fair order of difficulty in the index to the Sonatas.

The Beethoven Sonata with a Pastoral Character My teacher calls the Sonata opus 28, by Beethoven, the "Pastoral" Sonata. I have not found anything "pastoral" in any of the movements. Is it because I do not understand it, or is the name a mere amateurish invention?

The name "Pastoral Sonata" could, no doubt, be traced to an arbitrary invention, perhaps of some over-smart publisher endeavouring to heighten the attractiveness of the Sonata to the general public by the addition of a suggestive title. Yet it seems to fit the Sonata pretty well, because, really, its main characteristic is a rural sort of peaceful repose. Especially the first movement is of a tranquillity which, surely, does not suggest the life of a metropolis. But in the other movements, too, there are many episodes which by their naïveté and good-natured boisterousness indicate the life of the village.

Must I play all the Sonatas of Beethoven's in order to become a good player, or is a certain number of them sufficient, and, if so, how many would you advise? *A Few, Well Played, Are Enough*

Since the playing of all the Sonatas does not necessarily prove that they were all well played, I think it is better to play one Sonata well than to play many of them badly. Nor should Beethoven's Sonatas be regarded as a musical drilling-ground, but rather as musical revelations. As they are not all on precisely the same high plane of thought, it is not necessary to play them all. To familiarize yourself with Beethoven's style and grandeur of thought it is sufficient to have mastered six or eight of his Sonatas; though that number, at least, should be *mastered*.

MENDELSSOHN

In a complete course for a piano student should the study of Mendelssohn be included? Which of his compositions are the most useful? *The Study of Mendelssohn*

Mendelssohn is surely a composer who is not to be omitted. His melody alone, besides other virtues, entitles him to be included, for melody seems to grow scarce nowadays. To develop a fine cantilena his "Songs Without Words" of slower motion, for instance, are just the thing.

CHOPIN

What Is the Best of Chopin? Which are the best compositions of Chopin to study by one who really desires to know him?

All the Etudes, all the Preludes, the Ballades in A flat, G minor and F minor, the Berceuse and the Barcarolle. The Mazurkas, Nocturnes, Waltzes, and Polonaises you are probably familiar with; hence, I mention the aforesaid other works. Generally speaking, of Chopin a pianist should know everything.

The Charm of Chopin's Touch What kind of touch did Chopin have? Since a description of his touch would require too much space I refer you to the book from which I gathered the most explicit information on this point. It is "The Life of Chopin," by Frederick

Niecks (London and New York, No-
vello, Ewer & Co.), and in the second
volume, from page 94 to about 104, you
will find what you wish to know, as far
as it is possible to convey the charm of
one art through the medium of another.
Since you seem interested in Chopin
I would recommend that you closely
study both volumes of this masterly
biographical work.

What is the tempo (by metronome) *Mood*
of Chopin's Impromptu in A-flat, and *and*
Tempo in
what idea did the composer embody in it? *the A-Flat*
The editions vary in their metronome *Impromptu*
markings and I believe none of them.
Your tempo will largely depend upon
the state of your technique. To the
second question my reply is that Chopin
has composed "music" which — as you
know — represents thoughts only in a
musical sense, otherwise it deals with
purely psychic processes, moods, etc.
The humour of this Impromptu is mainly
an amiable, ingratiating one, here and
there slightly tinged with a sweet melancholy. It should not be played too fast,
for it easily loses this latter attribute

and then sounds like a Czerny exercise.
A moderate tempo will also tend to bring
out the many charming harmonic turns
which, in too quick a tempo, are likely
to be lost.

Chopin's
Barcarolle
In Chopin's Barcarolle there is a
number of trills preceded by grace notes.
Are they to be executed according to
Philipp Emmanuel Bach's rule, so that
the grace notes take their time from the
note that follows them?

Philipp Emmanuel Bach's rule is a
safe one to follow, but do not confound
a rule with a law. If you have reached
that plane on which an attempt at the
Barcarolle by Chopin is rational, you
must feel that your individual taste will
not lead you too far astray even if it
should prompt you occasionally to depart
from the rule.

Chopin's
Works
for a
Popular
Concert
What works of Chopin would you
suggest for a popular concert programme?
Nocturne, Opus 27, No. 2; Fantasy
Impromptu, Opus 66; Scherzo, Opus 31;
Berceuse, Opus 57; Valse, Opus 64, No.
2; Polonaise, Opus 26, No. 1; Chants
Polonais (in Liszt's transcription).

In playing Chopin may one take *Taking* liberties with the tempo and play different *Liberties with the* parts of the same mazurka or nocturne *Tempo* in various degrees of tempo?

Undoubtedly. But the extent of such liberties depends upon your æsthetic training. In principle your question admits of an affirmative reply, but a specific answer is impossible without an acquaintance with your musical status. I recommend that you be very cautious about "taking liberties"; without, however, ceasing altogether to follow the promptings of your good taste here and there. There is such a thing as "artistic conscience"; consult it always before taking a liberty with the tempo.

In the beginning of the Waltz in E *Omitting* minor by Chopin the left hand has to *One Note in a Chord* play this chord   a number of times. I can   stretch any three of the   four notes, but not all four.   Can one of them be omitted, and which one?

You may omit the upper E, the second note from the top, but you may do so only so long as it is physically impossible for you to strike all the four notes. For, by omitting this note you do alter the tone colour of the chord as well as its sonority. As soon as you have acquired the requisite stretch — and anybody who does possess it — I would advise that the note be not unnecessarily omitted. Chopin evidently meant to have that note played.

Masters Cannot be Studied in Order Will you give me your views as to the order in which the masters of piano composition should be studied?

To classify composers, without specifying their works, is never advisable. Beethoven's first and last sonatas differ so fundamentally from each other in every particular that one may play the first one very well and yet be for many years (perhaps forever) unable to play the last one. And still, it is the same Beethoven that wrote both works. We can, therefore, hardly speak of an "order of composers." So long as we are dealing with masters the question should not be: Which master? — but, Which composition does your stage of mental and technical development call for? If you will defer the study of any other composer until you have fully mastered the works of Beethoven — only the principal ones, at that — you will need a life of more length than the Bible allots to the average man.

Is it true that nearly all the great composers have been pianists?

The Greatest Composers as Pianists

If by pianists you mean musicians whose sole medium of audible musical utterance was the piano, your question admits of no other than an affirmative reply. The only exception I can think of just now was Berlioz; there were, no doubt, others, but none who belongs to the truly great ones. The reason for this is, perhaps, the circumstance that the pianist throughout his education is brought into touch with greater polyphony than the players of other instruments, and that polyphony is a basic principle in music.

Is the study of Thalberg's operatic transcriptions of any value to the piano student?

The Study of Operatic Transcriptions

Operatic transcriptions begin with Liszt. What was written before him in that line (and in some degree contemporary with him, hence it includes Thalberg) is hardly of any significance. If you feel a special inclination toward the transcriptions of Thalberg you may play them; they will not harm you so very much. But if you ask me whether they are of any musical value I must frankly say, no.

Modern Piano Music   Are such pieces as "Beautiful Star of Heaven" or "Falling Waters" in good taste? What contemporary composers write good piano music?

Pieces with pretentious names are usually devoid of such contents as their names imply, so that the names are merely a screen to hide the paucity of thoughts and ideas. Speaking very generally, there seems to be not very much good music written for the piano just at present. By far the best comes from Russia. Most of these compositions are rather difficult to play, but there are some easy ones to be found among them, such as the "Music Box," by Liadow, "Fantastic Fairy Tales," No. 12, by Pachulski, and others.

EXERCISES AND STUDIES

Is there any special book of practice *Exercises* exercises that you think best for a beginner *for the* and that you would care to recommend? *to Prac-*

Any reliable music publisher will tell *tise* you which book of exercises is most in demand. The effect of the exercises depends, of course, upon the way you play them. Indications as to touch, etc., are usually given in such books. What kind of exercises your case demands cannot be determined without a personal examination by an expert.

What would you say are the best *Good* studies for plain finger work? *Finger*

The exercises of "Pischna" are to be *Exercises* recommended. They have appeared in two editions, or which one is abridged. They are known as the "large" and the "small Pischna." You may obtain them through any large music house, I think, in the Steingräber Edition.

Are Heller's studies practical for a *The Value* young student lacking in rhythm and *of Heller's* expression? *Studies*

Yes, they are very good, provided the

teacher insists that the pupil plays exactly what is indicated and does not merely "come near it."

Good Intermediate Books of Etudes Living in the country, where there is no teacher available, I would thank you for telling me what Etudes I ought to study. I have finished those by Cramer and Moscheles, and can play them well, but find those by Chopin too difficult. Are there no intermediate works?

You seem to be fond of playing Etudes. Well, then, I suggest:

"Twelve Etudes for Technique and Expression," by Edmund Neupert.

"Concert Etudes," by Hans Seeling (Peters Edition).

"Etudes," by Carl Baermann (two books), published in Germany.

"Etudes," by Ruthardt (Peters Edition).

But why not select an easy Etude by Chopin and make a start? The best preparation — if not the Etudes themselves — is Heller's Opus 154.

Etudes For Advanced Players to Work at What regular technical work would you prescribe for a fairly advanced pianist — one who plays pretty well such things as the Chopin Etudes in C minor, Opus 10, No. 12, and in D flat, Opus 25, No. 8, and the B flat minor prelude?

My advice to advanced players is always that they should construct their technical exercises out of such material as the different places in the pieces at hand furnish. If you should feel the need of Etudes for increasing your endurance and control of protracted difficult passages I suggest that you take up the Etudes by Baermann and those by Kessler. The former are a little easier than the latter.

My first teacher laid great store by Clementi's "Gradus ad Parnassum," and insisted upon taking every study in it, while my new teacher, with whom I recently started lessons, says that it is "outlived, superannuated." Was my old or my new teacher right? *The Value of Clementi's "Gradus" To-day*

They were both right; one as a pedagogue, the other as a musician. As you do not mention the reason of your first teacher's insistence, I must assume that he employed the "Gradus" as exercises, pure and simple. It serves this purpose

quite well, though even as studies for the
applying of technical disciplines they are,
on account of their dryness, "outlived,"
as your new teacher correctly says. Modern writers have produced studies which
combine with their technical usefulness
greater musical value and attractiveness.

POLYRHYTHMS

*Playing
Duple
Time
Against
Triple*

How must I execute triplets played
against two-eighths? In Clementi's Sonatina, Opus 37, No. 3, first page, you
will find such bars.

In a slow tempo it may serve you to
think of the second eighth-note of the
triplet as being subdivided into two
sixteenths. After both hands have played
the first note of their respective groups
simultaneously, the place of the aforesaid
second sixteenth is to be filled by the
second note of the couplet. In faster
motion it is far better to practise at first
each hand alone and with somewhat
exaggerated accents of each group until
the two relative speeds are well established in the mind. Then try to play
the two hands together in a sort of semi-
automatic way. Frequent correct repe-

tition of the same figure will soon change your semi-automatic state into a conscious one, and thus train your ear to listen to and control two different rhythms or groupings at the same time.

How should, in Chopin's Fantasy Impromptu, the four notes of the right be played to the three of the left? Is an exact division possible?

The Two Hands Playing Different Rhythms

An exact division would lead to such fractions as the musician has no means of measuring and no terms for expressing. There is but one way to play unequal rhythms simultaneously in both hands; study each hand separately until you can depend upon it, and put them together without thinking of either rhythm. Think of the points where the two hands have to meet, the "dead points" of the two motions, and rely on your automatism until, by frequent hearing, you have learned to listen to two rhythms at once.

The Old Problem of Duple Time Against Triple   How should the above-quoted notes be brought in with the lower triplets?

It would be futile to attempt a precise and conscious division in such cases. The best, in fact, the only, way to do is to practise the hands separately with an exaggerated accent on each beat until the points where the hands meet are well conceived and the relative speed ratios are well understood. Then try to play the hands together, and do not be discouraged if the first attempts fail. Repeat the trial often and you will finally succeed if the separate practice has been sufficient to produce a semi-automatic action of the hands.

PHRASING

The Value and Correct Practice of Phrasing   Can you give an amateur a concise definition of phrasing and a few helpful suggestions as to clear phrasing?

Phrasing is a rational division and subdivision of musical sentences, and serves to make them intelligible. It corresponds closely with punctuation in literature and its recitation. Find out the start, the end, and the culminating point of your phrase. The last-named

is usually to be found upon the highest
note of the phrase, while the former are
usually indicated by phrasing slurs. Generally speaking, the rising of the melody
is combined with an increase of strength
up to the point of culmination, where,
in keeping with the note design, the
decrease of strength sets in. For artistic
phrasing it is of the utmost importance
properly to recognize the principal mood
of the piece, for this must, naturally,
influence the rendition of every detail
in it. A phrase occurring in an agitated
movement, for instance, will have to be
rendered very differently from a similar-
looking phrase in a slow, dreamy movement.

In observing a rest should the hand be
raised from the wrist?

Do Not Raise Wrist in Marking a Rest

Never! Such a motion should be
made only in rapid wrist octaves or other
double notes when a staccato is prescribed.
The regular way to conclude a phrase, or
observe a pause, as you say, is to lift the
arm from the keyboard and keep the
wrist perfectly limp, so that the arm
carries the loosely hanging hand upward.

RUBATO

As to Playing Rubato   Will you please tell me what is the best method of playing rubato?

The artistic principles ruling rubato playing are good taste and keeping within artistic bounds. The physical principle is balance. What you shorten of the time in one phrase or part of a phrase you must add at the first opportunity to another in order that the time "stolen" (rubato) in one place may be restituted in another. The æsthetic law demands that the total time-value of a music piece shall not be affected by any rubato, hence, the rubato can only have sway within the limits of such time as would be consumed if the piece were played in the strictest time.

How to Play Passages Marked "Rubato"   I find an explanation of *tempo rubato* which says that the hand which plays the melody may move with all possible freedom, while the accompanying hand must keep strict time. How can this be done?

The explanation you found, while not absolutely wrong, is very misleading, for it can find application only in a very few isolated cases; only inside of one short phrase and then hardly satisfactorily. Besides, the words you quote are not an explanation, but a mere assertion or, rather, allegation. *Tempo rubato* means a wavering, a vacillating of time values, and the question whether this is to extend over both hands or over only one must be decided by the player's good taste; it also depends upon whether the occupation of the two hands can be thought of as separate and musically independent. I assume that you are able to play each hand alone with perfect freedom, and I doubt not that you can, with some practice, retain this freedom of each hand when you unite them, but I can see only very few cases to which you could apply such skill, and still less do I see the advantage thereof.

In playing *rubato* do you follow a preconceived notion or the impulse of the moment?

Perfect Rubato the Result of Momentary Impulse

Perfect expression is possible only under perfect freedom. Hence, the perfect *rubato* must be the result of momentary impulse. It is, however, only a few very eminent players that have such command over this means of expression as to feel safe in trusting their momentary impulses altogether. The average player will do well carefully to consider the shifting of time values and to prepare their execution to a certain degree. This should not, however, be carried too far, as it would impair the naturalness of expression and lead to a stereotyped mannerism.

The Difference Between Conception and Rubato

Is there any difference between conception and *rubato*?

Conception is a generic term and comprises the service of each and all means of expression, among which *rubato* plays a somewhat prominent part. For it is, so to speak, the musical pulse-beat of the player. Being subordinate to conception, its function and manner must be governed by the latter.

CONCEPTION

Different Conceptions May be Individually Correct

Can one and the same phrase be conceived differently by different artists and still be individually correct in each instance ?

Certainly! Provided that — whatever the conception be — it preserves the logical relations of the parts in building up the phrase, and that it is carried through the whole course of the piece in a consistent manner. Whether a certain conception of a phrase is or is not compatible with the general character of the piece and how far the freedom of conception may extend, it will be for the æsthetic training and the good taste of the player to determine for each and every case separately.

In the first attempts at a new piece must matters of conception be observed at once or only after the piece has been technically mastered ?

Which Should Come First— Conception or Technique ?

Unless one is a very experienced reader it will be hardly possible to think of matters of conception until the technical means to express them and the necessary perspective of the piece have been gained. It is always safer first to make sure that the notes as such, and their respective times value have been read correctly, and that the technical difficulties have, to a fair degree, been overcome. This done, the question must be settled as to whether the general character

of the piece is dramatic, *i. e.*, tragic
or conciliatory, melancholy, lyric, rhap-
sodic, humorous, or changeable, and so
forth. Only when our mind on this
point is made up with the utmost definiteness, can we approach the details that
are conditioned by the conception.

FORCE OF EXAMPLE

Hearing a Piece Before Studying It   Should a pupil hear a piece played
before studying it?

If the pupil's imagination needs stimu-
lation he should hear the piece well
played before studying it. If, however,
he is merely too lazy to find out the
rhythm, melody, and so forth, and rather
relies upon his purely imitative faculty,
he should not hear it, but be compelled
to do his own reading and thinking.

THEORY

Why the Pianist Should Study Harmony   Do you recommend the study of harmony
and counterpoint to the piano student?

By all means! To gain a musical
insight into the pieces you play you
must be able to follow the course of their
harmonies and understand the contrapuntal treatment of their themes. With-

out the knowledge gained through a serious study of harmony and counter-point your conceptions will be pure guesswork and will lack in outline and definiteness.

Why is it supposed to be necessary to have fifteen keys to complete the circle of fifths? Why would not twelve suffice, and thus avoid duplicate keys? *Why so Many Different Keys?*

Not fifteen, but twenty-five tonalities complete the circle of fifths, theoretically, and they are all necessary because of the many harmonic turns that occur in modern music and which could not be intelligently demonstrated unless we use the tonalities with seven, eight, nine or more sharps and flats. For otherwise we might have to change the signature so frequently as to become utterly confusing to even the most musicianly reader. C-sharp minor has but four sharps, yet the scale of its dominant (its next relative) has eight sharps.

Is it absolutely necessary for me to study harmony in connection with my piano? My teacher wants me to do it, but I don't see the use! Of what benefit is harmony? *The Relation of Harmony to Piano-Playing*

Of what benefit is the general school-work a child has to go through? To play the piano well a good hand and so many hours of practice are not sufficient; it requires a general musical education. This means, first and foremost, a knowledge of harmony, to which you may later add the study of counterpoint and forms. Your teacher is absolutely right.

Text-Books on Har-mony Would you care to recommend two or three of the best books on the study of harmony?

The doctrine of harmony is ever the same, but the modes of teaching it are constantly changing and, I trust, improving. For this reason I feel a certain hesitation in recommending at this time the text-books which I studied many years ago, especially as I am not certain that they have been translated into English. I advise you, therefore, to inquire of some good teacher of harmony or, at least, of a reliable music publisher or dealer. E. F. Richter and Bussler wrote works of recognized merit, which, though no longer modern, may be safely studied.

Is it possible to learn modulating from a book without the aid of a teacher, so as to connect two pieces of different tonality? *Learning to Modulate*

Possible, yes, but not probable; for since in your written exercises you are likely to err at times, you will need some one to point out your errors and so show you the way to correct them. Generally speaking, I do not think much of studying the rudiments of anything without the aid of an experienced adviser.

Is it possible to study counterpoint without a teacher, and, if so, what book can you recommend for its study? *Studying Counterpoint by One's Self*

It is quite possible, provided you are certain never to misunderstand your text-book and never to commit any errors. Otherwise you will need the advice of an experienced musician in correcting them. A good teacher, however, is always better than a book for this study. Of text-books there are a great many. Any reliable music house will furnish you with a list of them.

Should Piano Students Try to Compose? Besides my study of the piano shall I try to compose if I feel the inclination and believe I have some talent for it?

The practice of constructing will always facilitate your work of reconstructing, which is, practically, what the rendition of a musical work means. Hence, I advise every one who feels able to construct even a modest little piece to try his hand at it. Of course, if you can write only a two-step it will not enable you to reconstruct a Beethoven Sonata; still, there may be little places in the Sonata that will clear up in your mind more quickly when you have come in touch with the technical act of putting down on paper what your mind has created, and you will altogether lose the attitude of the absolute stranger when facing a new composition. Do not construe this, however, as an encouragement to write two-steps!

The Student Who Wants to Compose Please advise me as to the best way of learning composition. Which is the best work of that kind from which I could learn?

First learn to write notes. Copying

all sorts of music is the best practice for
that. Then study the doctrine of harmony. Follow it up by a study of the
various forms of counterpoint. Proceed
to canon in its many kinds and intervals.
Take up the fugue. Then study forms
until you learn to feel them. Books for
every one of these stages there are many,
but better than all the books is a good
teacher.

What is the difference between the *The*
major and minor scale? Does it lie in *Difference Between*
the arrangement of semitones or in the *Major*
character, or in both? *and*
Minor
There are three differences: First, in *Scales*
the arrangement of the semitones; second,
in the character; and, third, in the circumstance that the minor scale admits
of a number of modifications for melodic
purposes which cannot be made in the
major scale.

Which is the true minor scale, the *There is*
melodic or the harmonic? My teacher *Only One Minor*
insists upon the harmonic, but it sounds *Scale*
ugly to me. Will you please tell me
something about it?

There is but one minor scale; it is the one upon which the chords of its tonality are built; it is the one upon which your teacher wisely insists, because the so-called melodic minor scale offers no new intervals to your fingers, and because the term melodic minor scale is applied to that form of deviation from the real scale which is most frequently used, but which is by no means the only deviation that is possible; nor is it the only one in use.

What is the Difference Between the Major and Minor Scales? What is the difference between the major and minor scales?

The major scale has a major third and sixth, while the minor scale has a minor third and sixth and raises its seventh to a major seventh by an accidental elevating sign, raising a natural note by a sharp, and a flat note by a natural. If you begin your major scale upon its sixth degree and, counting it as the first of the minor, raise the seventh, you obtain the minor scale, in which, however, many modifications are admissible for melodic (though not for harmonic) purposes.

As a waltz and a menuet are both in three-fourth time, is it only the tempo in which they differ, or are there other differences?

How Waltz, Menuet, Mazurka, and Polonaise Differ

Waltz, menuet, mazurka, and polonaise are all in three-fourth time and are not confined to a definite tempo. The difference between them lies in the structure. A waltz period — that is, the full expression of a theme — needs sixteen measures; a menuet needs only eight, a mazurka only four measures. In a mazurka a motive occupies only one measure, in the menuet two, and in the waltz four. The polonaise subdivides its quarters into eighths, and the second eighth usually into two sixteenths ; it differs, therefore, from the other three dances by its rhythm.

What is the meaning of the word "Toccata"? I do not find it in the Italian lexicon and the English musical dictionaries differ widely in their definitions. None of their definitions seems to apply to the Toccata by Chaminade.

The Meaning of "Toccata"

To make the matter quite plain let me say, first, that "Cantata" (from *cantare* — to sing) meant in olden times a music piece to be sung; while "Sonata" (from *suonare* — to play) designated a piece to be played on an instrument; and "Toccato" meant a piece for keyboard instruments like the organ or piano and its precursors, written with the intention of providing special opportunities for the display of the skill of touch (from *toccare* — to touch) or, as we would now say, finger technique. The original meanings have changed so that these terms now imply definite forms, like the modern Cantata and Sonata. The Toccata is, at present, understood to be a piece in constant and regular motion, very much like those that are called "*moto perpetuo*" or "perpetual motion," of which Weber's "Perpetuum mobile" is a good example. I have no doubt that the Toccata by Chaminade, which I do not know, is written on similar lines.

THE MEMORY

Playing from Memory Is Indispensable   Is memorization absolutely essential to a good player?

Playing from memory is indispensable to the freedom of rendition. You have to bear in your mind and memory the whole piece in order to attend properly to its details.   Some renowned players who take the printed sheets before them on the stage play, nevertheless, from memory. They take the music with them only to heighten their feeling of security and to counteract a lack of confidence in their memory — a species of nervousness.

Will you please tell me which is the easiest way to memorize a piano piece ? *The Easiest Way to Memorize*

Begin by playing it a few times very carefully and slowly until you can play it with a fair degree of exactitude (you need not mind an occasional stopping). Then go over such places as appeared to you especially complex until you understand their construction.   Now let the piece rest for a whole day and try to trace in your mind the train of thoughts in the piece.   Should you come to a dead stop be satisfied with what you have achieved.   Your mind will keep on working, subconsciously, as over a puzzle, always trying to find the continuation. If you find that the memory is a blank take the music in hand, look at the particular place — but only at this — and, since you have now found the connection, continue the work of mental tracing. At the next stop repeat this procedure until you have reached the end, not in every detail, but in large outlines. Of course, this does not mean that you can now *play* it from memory. You have only arrived at the point of transition from the imagined to the real, and now begins a new kind of study: to transfer to the instrument what you have mentally absorbed. Try to do this piece by piece, and look into the printed sheets (which should not be on the music-rack but away from it) only when your memory absolutely refuses to go on. The real work with the printed music should be reserved to the last, and you should regard it in the light of a proof-reading of your mental impressions. The whole process of absorbing a piece of music mentally resembles that of photographing. The development of the acoustic picture (the tone-picture) is like the bath. The tentative playing is like the process of "fixing" against sensitiveness to lights; and the final work with the printed music is the retouching.

I find it very hard to memorize my music. Can you suggest any method that would make it easier? *In Order to Memorize Easily*

To retain in one's memory what does not interest one is difficult to everybody, while that which does interest us comes easy. In your case the first requirement seems to be that your interest in the pieces you are to play be awakened. This interest usually comes with a deeper understanding of music; hence, it may be said that nothing will assist a naturally reluctant memory so much as a general musical education. Special studies for the memory have not come to my knowledge because I never had any need of them. After all, the best way to memorize is — to memorize. One phrase to-day, another to-morrow, and so on, until the memory grows by its own force through being exercised.

I memorize very easily, so that I can often play my pieces from memory before I have fully mastered their technical difficulties, as my teacher *Memorizing Quickly and Forgetting as Readily* says. But I forget them just as quickly, so that in a few weeks I cannot remember enough of them to play them clear through. What would you advise, to make my memory more retentive?

There are two fundamental types of memory: One is very mobile — it acquires quickly and loses just as quickly; the other is more cumbrous in its action — it acquires slowly, but retains forever. A combination of the two is very rare, indeed; I never heard of such a case. A remedy against forgetting you will find in refreshing your memory in regular periods, playing your memorized pieces over (carefully) every four or five days. Other remedies I know not and I see no necessity for them.

To Keep Errors from Creeping in   I can always memorize a piece before I can play it fast. Do you advise practising with notes when I already know it by heart?

The occasional playing of a memorized piece from the notes will keep errors from creeping in, provided you read the music correctly and carefully.

SIGHT READING

Is there any practical method that will assist one to greater rapidity in sight-reading? *The Best Way to Improve Sight-Reading*

The best way to become a quick reader is to read as much as possible. The rapidity of your progress depends upon the state of your general musical education, for the more complete this is the better you will be able to surmise the logical sequel of a phrase once started. A large part of sight-reading consists of surmising, as you will find upon analyzing your book-reading.

What is a good plan to pursue to improve the facility in sight-reading? *To Gain Facility in Sight-Reading*

Much reading and playing at sight and as fast as possible, even though at first some slight inaccuracies may creep in. By quick reading you develop that faculty of the eye which is meant by "grasp," and this, in turn, facilitates your reading of details.

ACCOMPANYING

How can one learn to accompany at sight? *Learning to Accompany at Sight*

Develop your sight-reading by playing

many accompaniments, and endeavour — while playing your part — also to read and inwardly hear the solo part.

The Art of Accompanying a Soloist   How should one manage the accompaniment for a soloist inclined to play rubato ?

Since you cannot make a contract of artistically binding force with a soloist you must take refuge in "following." But do not take this word in its literal meaning; rather endeavour to divine the intentions of your soloist from moment to moment, for this divining is the soul of accompanying. To be, in this sense, a good accompanist, one must have what is called in musical slang a good "nose" — that is, one must musically "scent" whither the soloist is going. But, then, the nose is one of the things we are born with. We may develop it, as to its sensitiveness, but we cannot acquire a nose by learning. Experience will do much in these premises, but not everything.

Learning the Art of Accompanying   Wishing to become an accompanist I anticipate completing my studies in Berlin. What salary might I expect and what would be the best "course" to pursue ?

An experienced and very clever accompanist may possibly earn as much as fifty dollars a week if associated with a vocal, violin, or 'cello artist of great renown. Usually, however, accompanists are expected to be able to play solos. There are no special schools for accompanists, though there may be possibly some special courses in which experience may be fostered. If you come to Berlin you will find it easy to find what you seem to be seeking.

TRANSPOSING

What, please, is the quickest and safest way of transposing from one key to another? I have trouble, for instance, in playing for singing if the piece is in A major and the singer wants it in F major.

The Problem of Transposing at Sight

The question of transposing hinges on the process of hearing through the eye. I mean by this that you must study the piece until you learn to conceive the printed music as sounds and sound groups, not as key pictures. Then transfer the sound picture to another tonality in your mind, very much as if when moving from one floor to another with all your household goods you were to place them on the new floor as they were placed on the old. Practice will, of course, facilitate this process very much. Transposition at sight is based on somewhat different principles. Here you have to get mentally settled in the new tonality, and then follow the course of intervals. If you find transposition difficult you may derive consolation from the thought that it is difficult for everybody, and that transposing at sight is, of course, still more difficult than to transpose after studying the piece beforehand.

PLAYING FOR PEOPLE

When to "Play For People" During the period of serious study may I play for people (friends or strangers) or should I keep entirely away from the outside world?

From time to time you may play for people the pieces you have mastered, but take good care to go over them afterward — the difficult places slowly — in order to eliminate any slight errors or unevenness that may have crept in. To play for people is not only a good incentive for further aspirations; it also furnishes you with a fairly exact estimate of your abilities and shortcomings, and indicates thereby the road to improvement. To retire from the outside world during the period of study is an outlived, obsolete idea which probably originated in the endeavour to curb the vanity of such students as would neglect their studies in hunting, prematurely, for applause. I recommend playing for people moderately and on the condition that for every such "performance" of a piece you play it afterward twice, slowly and carefully, at home. This will keep the piece intact and bring you many other unexpected advantages.

I can never do myself justice when playing for people, because of my nervousness. How can I overcome it?

"Afraid to Play Before People"

If you are absolutely certain that your trouble is due to "nervousness" you should improve the condition of your nerves by proper exercise in the open air and by consulting your physician. But are you quite sure that your "nervousness" is not merely another name for self-consciousness, or, worse yet, for a "bad conscience" on the score of technical security? In the latter case you ought to perfect your technique, while in the former you must learn to discard all thought of your dear self, as well as of your hearers in relation to you, and concentrate your thinking upon the work you are to do. This you can well achieve by will-power and persistent self-training.

Effect of Playing the Same Piece Often I have heard artists play the same piece year after year, and each time as expressively as before. After a piece has been played several hundred times it can hardly produce on the player the same emotional effect that it originally did. Is it possible for a player by his art and technical resources so to colour his tones that he can stimulate and produce in his audience an emotional condition which he himself does not at the time feel?

In music emotion can be conveyed only through the means and modes of expression that are peculiar to music, such as dynamic changes, vacillations of tempo, differences of touch and kindred devices. When a piece is played in public very often on consecutive occasions — which artists avoid as much as they can — these expressions gradually assume a distinct form which is quite capable of preservation. Though it will in time lose its life-breath, it can still produce a deception just as (to draw a drastic parallel) a dead person may look as if he were only asleep. In this parallel the artist has, however, one great advantage. Since he cannot play a piece very often without having a number of errors, rearrangements, slight changes creeping into it, he must, in order to eliminate them and to cleanse the piece, return from time to time to slow practice in which he also refrains almost entirely from expression. When in the next public performance the right tempo and expression are added again they tend strongly to renew the freshness of the piece in the player's mind.

I love music dearly and my teacher is always satisfied with my lessons, but when I play for my friends I never make a success. They compliment me, but I feel they that do not care for my playing; even my mother says that my playing is "mechanical." How can I change it?

The Pianist Who Fails to Express Herself

It is just possible that your friends and your mother may not be amenable to the high class of music which you play, but if this is not the case your affliction cannot be cured offhand. If the lack of expression in your playing should emanate from a lack of feeling in yourself, then your case would be incurable. If, however, you play "mechanically" because you do not know how to express your emotions in your playing — and I suspect it to be so — then you are curable, although there are no remedies that would act directly. I suggest that you form close associations with good musicians and with lovers of good music. By looking well and listening you can learn their modes of expression and employ them first by imitation until the habit of "saying something" when you play has grown upon you. I think, though, that you need an inward change before there can be any outward change.

The Art of Playing With Feeling In the musical manifestations of feeling how does the artist chiefly differ from the amateur?

The artist expresses his feelings with due deference to the canons of art. Above all, he plays correctly without allowing this ever-present correctness to make his playing seem lacking in feeling. Without unduly repressing or suppressing his individuality he respects the composer's intentions by punctiliously obeying every hint or suggestion he finds in the annotations, concerning speed, force, touch, changes, contrasts, etc. He delivers the composer's message truthfully. His personality or individuality reveals itself solely in the way he understands the composition and in the manner in which he executes the composer's prescriptions.

Not so the amateur. Long before he is able to play the piece correctly he begins to twist and turn things in it to suit himself, under the belief, I suppose, that he is endowed with an "individuality" so strong as to justify an indulgence in all manner of "liberties," that is, licence. Feeling is a great thing; so is the will to express it; but both are worthless without ability. Hence, before playing with feeling, it were well to make sure that everything in the piece is in the right place, in the right time, strength, touch, and so forth. Correct reading — and not only of the notes *per se* — is a matter that every good teacher insists upon with his pupils, even in the earliest grades of advancement. The amateur should make sure of that before he allows his "feelings" to run riot. But he very seldom does.

Affected Movements at the Piano   Is there any justification for the swaying of the body, the nodding of the head, the exaggerated motion of the arms, and all grotesque actions in general while playing the piano, so frequently exhibited not only by amateurs but by concert players, too?

All such actions as you describe reveal a lack of the player's proper self-control when they are unconsciously indulged in. When they are consciously committed, which is not infrequently the case, they betray the pianist's effort to deflect the auditors' attention from the composition to himself, feeling probably unable to satisfy his auditors with the result of his playing and, therefore, resorting to illustration by more or less exaggerated gesture. General well-manneredness, or its absence, has a good deal to do with the matter.

ABOUT THE PIANO PER SE

Do you believe that the piano is the most difficult of all instruments to master — more so than the organ or the violin? If so, why?

Is the Piano the Hardest to Master?

The piano is more difficult to master than the organ, because the tone-production on the piano is not so purely mechanical as it is on the organ. The pianist's touch is the immediate producer of whatever variety or colour of tone the moment requires, whereas the organist is powerless to produce any change of tone colour except by pulling a different stop. His fingers do not and cannot produce the change. As to string instruments, their difficulties lie in an entirely different field, and this fact precludes comparison with the piano. Technically, the string instrument may be more difficult, but to become an exponent of musical art on the piano requires deeper study, because the pianist must present to his hearers the totality of a composition while the string instruments depend for the most part upon the accompaniments of some other instruments.

Piano Study for Conductor and Composer

Being a cornet player, and wishing to become a conductor and composer, I should like to know if the study of the piano is necessary in addition to my broad, theoretical studies and a common college course.

It depends upon what you wish to conduct and what to compose. With no other means of musically expressing yourself than a cornet it is highly improbable that you will be able to write or conduct a symphony. But you may be able to lead a brass band and, perhaps, to write a march or dance piece. If your musical aims are serious by all means take to the piano.

Why the Piano Is So Popular

Why do more people play the piano than any other instrument?

Because the rudimentary stages of music study are easier on the piano than on any other instrument. The higher stages, however, are so much more difficult, and it is then that the piano gets even with the bold aggressor. A violinist or 'cellist who can play a melody simply and with good tone is considered a fairly good amateur, for he must have mastered the difficulty of tone-production; he must have trained his right arm. A pianist who can play a melody equally well is the merest tyro. When he approaches polyphony, when the discrimination begins between the various parts speaking simultaneously, aye, then the real work begins — not to speak of velocity. It is, perhaps, for this reason that in reality there are a great many more violinists than pianists, if by either we mean persons who really master their instrument. The number of 'cellists is smaller, but the reason for this is to be found in the small range of 'cello literature and also, perhaps, in the comparative unwieldiness of the instrument, which does not admit of technical development as, for instance, the more handy violin. If all beginners at the piano realized what exasperating, harassing, discouraging, nerve-consuming difficulties await them later and beset the path to that mastery which so few achieve, there would be far fewer piano students and more people would study the violin or the 'cello. Of the harp and the wind instruments I need not speak, because they are to be considered only in matters orchestral and not — seriously — as solo instruments.

The Genuine Piano Hand What shape of hand do you consider the best for piano playing? Mine is very broad, with rather long fingers.

The best piano hand is not the popular, pretty, narrow hand with long fingers. Nearly all the great technicians had or have proportioned hands. The genuine piano hand must be broad, in order to give each finger a strong base for the action of its phalanges and to give this base space enough for the development of the various sets of muscles. The length of the fingers must be in proportion to the width of the hand, but it is the width which I consider most important.

The Composition Must Fit the Player Would you advise players with small hands to attempt the heavier class of compositions by Liszt?

Never! Whether the hands are too

small or the stretch between the fingers too narrow — if you attempt a piece which for these or other physical reasons you cannot fully master, you always run the serious risk of overstraining. This, however, should be most carefully avoided. If you cannot play a certain piece without undue physical strain, leave it alone and remember that singers choose their songs not because they lie within their compass, but because they suit their voice. Do likewise. Be guided by the nature and the type of your hand rather than by its rapidity of execution.

The Best Physical Exercise for the Pianist

What physical exercises are most advantageous to be taken in connection with piano practice? I have been swinging clubs to strengthen wrists and arms, but have imagined it stiffened my fingers.

I am inclined to think that what you imagined was not far from the truth. Can you not replace the real clubs by imaginary ones? Since club-swinging tends to develop the agility of the arms and wrists rather than their strength you can easily make the same motions without the clubs; for all exertion of force that keeps the hands in a closed condition is bound to have a bad effect on piano playing. Undoubtedly the best exercise of all, however, is brisk walking in the open air, for it engages every part and every organ of the body, and by compelling deep breathing it fosters the general health through increased oxygenation.

Horseback Riding Stiffens the Fingers   My teacher objects to my riding horseback; not altogether, but he says I overdo it and it stiffens my fingers. Is he right?

Yes, he is. Every abuse carries its own punishment in its train. The closed position of the hand, the pressure of the reins upon the fingers, as constant as it is the case in horseback riding, is surely not advantageous for the elasticity of the fingers. You should, therefore, allow the effect of one ride upon your fingers to disappear completely before you indulge in another.

When to Keep Away from the Piano   Do you think I should play and study the piano just because it is asked of me, and when I take no interest in it?

Most emphatically, no! It would be

a crime against yourself and against
music. What little interest in music
you may have left would be killed by
a study that is distasteful to you, and
this would be, therefore, bound to lead
to failure. Leave this study to people
who are sincerely interested in it. Thank
heaven, there are still some of those, and
there always will be some! Be sure,
however, that you are really not interested,
and discriminate well between a lack of
interest and a mere opposition to a
perhaps too strenuous urging on the part
of your relatives. My advice would be
to quit the study for a time entirely; if,
after a while, you feel a craving for
music you will find the way to your
instrument. This advice, of course, holds
good also for violin students or any type
of music student.

BAD MUSIC

Must I persist in playing classical *The*
pieces when I prefer to play dance music? *Company That One*
If, in your daily life, you wish to be *Keeps in*
regarded as a lady or a gentleman you *Music*
are obliged to be careful as to the company
you keep. It is the same in musical life.

If you associate with the noble thoughts that constitute good — or, as you call it, classical — music, you will be counted with a higher class in the world of music. Remember that you cannot go through a flour-mill without getting dusty. Of course, not all pieces of dance music are bad; but the general run of them are such poor, if not vulgar, stuff as hardly to deserve the name of "compositions." Usually they are mere "expositions" of bad taste. Of these I warn you for your own sake, and if you wish to avoid the danger of confounding the good and the bad in that line it is best to abstain from it entirely. If dance music it must be, why, have you never heard of the waltzes and mazurkas by Chopin?

Why Rag-Time Is Injurious Do you believe the playing of the modern rag-time piece to be actually hurtful to the student?

I do, indeed, unless it is done merely for a frolic; though even such a mood might vent itself in better taste. The touch with vulgarity can never be but hurtful, whatever form vulgarity may assume — whether it be literature, a person, or a piece of music. Why share the musical food of those who are, by breeding or circumstance, debarred from anything better? The vulgar impulse which generated rag-time cannot arouse a noble impulse in response any more than "dime novels" can awaken the instincts of gentlemanliness or ladyship. If we watch the street-sweeper we are liable to get dusty. But remember that the dust on the mind and soul is not so easily removed as the dust on our clothes.

ETHICAL

How can we know that our talent is great enough to warrant us in bestowing year after year of work upon its development? *What the Object of Study Should Be*

Pleasure and interest should be such that it is in the actual working that one is repaid. Do not think so much of the end of your work. Do not force your work with the one view of becoming a great artist. Let Providence and the future decide your standing in music. Go on studying with earnestness and interest, and find your pleasure in the endeavour, not in the accomplishment.

PITCH AND KINDRED MATTERS

The International Pitch   What is meant by "pitch" as regards piano tuning? People say that a certain piano is pitched lower than another. Would E on one piano actually sound like F on another?

Yes, it would if the pianos were not pitched alike. It is only recently that an international pitch has been established which was adopted everywhere except in England. In the international pitch the A in the second space of the treble staff makes 435 vibrations a second.

The "International" Piano Pitch   Which piano pitch is preferable, "concert" or "international"?

By all means the "international," because it will fit your piano to be used in conjunction with any other instrument, no matter whence it may come. Besides, the international pitch was decided upon as far back as 1859, in Paris, by a government commission, numbering among its members such men as Auber, Halévy, Berlioz, Meyerbeer, Rossini, Ambroise Thomas, and many physicists and army generals. You can easily infer from this that, in determining that the

A in the second space of the treble staff should have 435 vibrations a second, all phases of music — vocal, instrumental, string, brass, wood, wind — have been duly considered.

Is there really a difference of three-eighths of a tone between A-sharp and B-flat on the piano?

The Well-Tempered Piano Scale

There is no difference on the piano. But acoustically there is a difference, over which, however, I would waste no time, since the evenly-tempered scale has been generally adopted, and every composition from Bach's time to the present day has been thought and written in it.

Is it not a mistaken idea that any one particular key is more or less rich or melodious than another?

The "Colour" of Various Keys

The effect of a tonality upon our hearing lies not in its signature (as even Beethoven seemed to believe) but in the vibration proportions. It is, therefore, irrelevant whether we play a piece upon a high-pitched piano in C, or upon a low-pitched piano in D flat. There are certain keys preferable to others for certain colours, but I fear that the preference is based not upon acoustic qualities but rather upon a fitness for the hand or voice. We apply the word "colour" as much to tone as the painters apply "tone" to colour, but I hardly think that anybody would speak of C major as representing black, or F major green.

THE STUDENT'S AGE

Starting a Child's Musical Training At what age should a child begin the study of instrumental music? If my daughter (six years old) is to study the violin should she first spend a few years with the piano, or *vice versa?*

The usual age for a child to begin the study of music is between six and seven years. A pianist hardly needs to learn another instrument to become a well-rounded musician, but violinists, as well as the players of all other instruments, and also vocalists, will be much hampered in their general musical development if they fail to acquire what may be called a speaking acquaintance with the piano.

I am not longer in my first youth, *Age of the* cannot take more than one hour's lesson *Student is* a week, and cannot practise more than *Immaterial* three hours a day. Would you still advise me to begin the study of the piano?

Provided there is gift and intelligence, the will, and the opportunity to study, age need not stand in your way. If your three hours of study are properly used, and your hour's lesson a week is with a good teacher, you should not become discouraged.

Do you think that mastery of the piano *Twenty-* is unlikely or impossible when the begin- *five Not* ner is twenty-five years of age? *Too Late* *to Begin*

It is neither unlikely nor impossible. Your age will to some degree handicap you, because from purely physical causes the elasticity of the fingers and wrists could be developed much more quickly if you were ten years younger. If, however, you are endowed with strong musical gifts in the abstract you will achieve results superior to those attained by younger people with less talent. In overcoming the difficulties due to a late beginning you will find great inward satisfaction, and your attainments are bound to be a source of joy to you.

TEACHERS, LESSONS AND METHODS

The Importance of the Right Teacher   I have a son who is very desirous of learning to play the piano. I have been advised that an ordinarily good teacher is good enough to begin with. Others tell me a beginner should get the best teacher possible. Which would you advise? I live in a small town.

The seriousness of your question is aggravated by the statement that you live in a small town, and that there is possibly no teacher of ability to be be found in your town. And yet it is only such a one that I can recommend for your son. For nothing is more dangerous for the development of a talent than a bad foundation. Many people have tried all their lives to rid themselves of the bad habits acquired from an ignorant teacher in the rudimentary stages of their studies, and have failed. I should advise you to try your best to send your boy to some near-by city where there is an excellent teacher.

Wishing to begin the study of the piano now, in my twenty-fourth year, just for the sake of my great love for music, and knowing not even the notes, is it necessary to go to an expensive teacher at once or would a cheaper teacher do for the beginning?

Nothing But the Best Will Do

If music is to be merely a pastime, and you content yourself with a minimum of knowledge, the cheaper teacher will do; but if you aspire to become musical in a better sense, why, by all means, apply to a teacher of the better class. The maxim: "For the beginning this or that is good enough," is one of the most harmful fallacies. What would you think of an architect who says: "For the foundation loam is good enough; we put a sandstone house over it, any way." Remember also, that the road a cheaper teacher has led you to take must usually be retraced when your aspirations rise toward the better in music.

Shall I take my lessons in a music school or from a private teacher?

Music Schools and Private Teachers

Music schools are very good for acquiring a general musical education.

For the higher study of an executive specialty (piano, violin, the voice, etc.) I should naturally prefer private instruction from a specialist, because he can give more attention to each individual pupil than is possible under the wholesale system followed, not by all, but by the majority of music schools. What I should advise would be a combination: General matters — harmony, counterpoint, forms, history, and æsthetics — in a music school; and private lessons for your specialty from a teacher who has an established name as an executive artist. The best music schools have such a man at their head, and in these you find the best combination.

Individual Teacher, or Conservatory? After taking lessons for five years and a half from a good teacher, would you advise a continuance with the individual teacher or attendance at a college of music or conservatory?

For a general musical education I always recommend a good music school or conservatory. For the study of the piano I think it best to take private lessons from an artist who is experienced both as an executant and as a teacher. Some music schools have such men on their staff, if not, indeed, at their head.

Having had twenty months' lessons and having now mastered Etudes by Berens, opus 61, by Heller, opus 47, and Smith's Octave Studies, do you think I am justified in continuing my lessons? *Where Outside Criticism Is Desirable*

Assuming that you have really "mastered" the works you mention I can only encourage you to continue your lessons; I would, however, advise you to obtain an experienced pianist's criticism in order to assure yourself that your idea of "mastering" is right.

Is there any preference as to sex in the question of choosing a piano teacher; in other words, is a woman teacher preferable for any reason for a girl and and a man teacher for a man? *The Sex of the Piano Teacher*

Your question does not admit of generalization from a purely musical point of view. It must be — on this premise — decided by the quality, not by the sex, of the teacher. A good feminine teacher is better than a bad masculine one, and *vice versa.* The question of sex does not enter into the matter. Of course, the greater number of eminent teachers are found on the masculine side.

Too Much "Method"   My recently engaged teacher says that the word "method" jars on her nerves. Kindly advise me whether a method is not the best thing for a novice, and, if so, which one?

Your teacher, while possibly a little over-sensitive, is not wrong. America is the most method-ridden country in the world. Most of the methods in vogue contain some good points — about a grain of truth to a ton of mere ballast. Your teacher's utterance makes me think that you were lucky in finding her, and that you have excellent reason to trust in her guidance.

What the Lesche-tizky Method Is   How does the Leschetizky method rank with other methods, and in what respect does it differ from them?

There are but two methods in all the arts: a good one and a bad one. Since you do not specify with what "other" methods you wish to compare that of

Leschetizky I cannot answer you with definiteness. There are, alas, so many "methods"! But the majority of them are based upon a deliberate disregard for that reverence which is due to great compositions and to the example of their rendition given by great interpreters. I have not studied with Leschetizky, but I think that he believes in a very low position of the hand and a sort of super-energetic tension of the tendons of the arms and hands.

Has a young pupil, after studying the piano irregularly for two months, tested fairly a teacher's ability? *Give Your Teacher a Fair Trial*

Of course not! Altogether I do not like the idea of a pupil's testing his teacher's ability, rather the reverse. He may possibly find his teacher unsympathetic, but even this matter he is apt to judge prematurely. In most cases of irregularly attended or poorly prepared lessons the lack of sympathy means nothing more than that the pupil is a trifler and the teacher's honesty of purpose is not to his taste.

*Either
Trust
Your
Teacher
or Get a
New One*
I have a "Piano Method," left over from lessons with my first teacher; it was very expensive, and I learned only a few pages of it. We moved to a different city and my new teacher objects to using the book, or, as she says, any such book. I do not know what to do about it, and would thank you for your advice.

When you apply to a teacher for instruction you must, first of all, decide in your own mind whether you have or have not absolute confidence in his ability. If you trust him you must do as you are advised to do; if not, you must apply to another teacher. A book, costing much or little, plays no part in the matter. By what you say of the new teacher, however, I am disposed to think that he is better than the first one.

*The
Proper
Course
For a
Little
Girl*
Commencing piano lessons with my seven-year-old daughter, should I devote my efforts to the development of the fingers and hands, or retard such development so as to keep pace with the expansion of the mind?

Your question is interesting. But if

your mind is clear on that point — and
it seems to be — that a one-sided development (in this case technical) is
dangerous to the "musical" talent of
your little daughter, why, then, your
little girl is, indeed, "out of danger."
Your very question is a credit to your
insight.

Is it better for a young student to take *Frequent*
one hour lesson or two half-hour lessons *Lessons*
a week? *and*
Shorter

Since young students are liable to form
bad habits it is essential that they should
come under the teacher's eye as frequently
as possible. Hence, it is preferable to
divide the hour into two equidistant parts.

Which plan is better for a child of *Number*
eleven or twelve years: to take a one-hour *of Lessons*
lesson or two half-hour lessons a week? *Depends*
on
The child's age is not the determining *Progress*
factor in this matter; it is his musical
status.

Is one lesson a week inadequate for *One*
a piano student? *Lesson a*
Week
It will be sufficient in the more advanced stages of piano study. In the

earlier stages, however, where the danger of forming bad habits is greatest, it is best to bring the pupil under his teacher's eye twice a week at the very least.

Better Not Give the Child "Modified Classics"   What little classics are best for a child after six months' lessons?

There are collections without number of facilitated or simplified arrangements of classic pieces, but I do not altogether approve of them.   Let the classics wait until the child is technically — and, above all, mentally — ripe to approach such works as they are written.

Can Music Be Studied in America?   Is it necessary for me to go to Europe to continue my music studies?

If you have very much money to spare, why not?   You will see much, also hear much — and some of it not quite so sublime as you anticipated — and, last but not least, you will have "studied abroad."   While this slogan still exercises a certain charm upon some people in America, their number is growing less year by year, because the public has begun to understand that the United States affords just as good instruction in music as Europe does. It has also been found out that to "study abroad" is by no means a guarantee of a triumphant return. Many a young student who went abroad as a lamb returned as a mutton-head. And why should there not be excellent teachers in America by this time? Even if you should insist upon a European teacher you can find many of the best in America. Is it not simpler that one teacher from Europe go to America to teach a hundred students than that a hundred students should make the trip for the sake of one teacher? I should advise you to stay where you are or go to Philadelphia, New York, or Boston, where you can find excellent teachers, native, resident Americans and foreigners. To quote a case in point, let me say that in Berlin I found Godowsky's pupils to be almost exclusively Americans. They came from various sections of America to study with him and with no one else. But during the eighteen years he spent in Chicago they did not seem to want him. Perhaps he was too near by! Why this self-deception? Without mentioning any names I assure you that there are many teachers in America now who, if they should go to Europe, would draw a host of students after them, and some of these excellent men I know personally. It is high time to put an end to the superstitious belief in "studying abroad."

MISCELLANEOUS QUESTIONS

Organiz- ing a Musi- cal Club   Please give me the name of a good book on musical history and advise me how to organize and conduct a musical club among my pupils. Also give me a name, please.

You will find the "History of Music," by Baltzell, a serviceable book. As a name for your club I suggest that of the patron saint of music — Saint Cecilia — perhaps, or that of a great composer. Ask the secretaries of a number of musical clubs for their constitutions and by-laws and then adapt these to your locality and circumstances. Make your pupils feel that it is their club and act, yourself, as secretary, if possible.

How to Get Music Published   Please explain how to go about publishing a piece of music, and also give the name of some good publishing houses.

It is very easy to publish a piece of music if the publisher sees any merit in it. Send your piece to any publishing house whose name you find on the title pages of your sheet music. The readers or advisers of the house will report to their chief as to the merit of your piece, and he will then decide and negotiate with you, if his decision is favourable. If he should not care for it he will return your manuscript and you may try some other house. I advise you, however, to obtain the opinion of a good musician before you send your piece to a publisher.

What is the difference between playing "in time" and playing "in rhythm"? *"Playing in Time" and "Playing in Rhythm"*

Playing in rhythm refers to the inner life of a composition — to its musical pulsation. Playing in time means the prompt arrival upon those points of repose which are conditioned by the rhythm.

I find great difficulty in playing anything that goes quick, though in a more moderate tempo I can play my pieces faultlessly. Every teacher I had promised to develop my speed, but they all *The Student Who Cannot Play Fast Music* failed.   Can you give me a hint how to overcome my difficulty?

Quickness of action, of motion, even of resolution, cannot be acquired by training alone; it must partly be inborn. I assume that your piano-playing is one phase of a general slowness. There is but one remedy for that. You have relied upon your teachers to develop your speed — you should have relied upon your own will-power. Try to will it and to will it often; you will see the ability keep step with the exertions of your will.

"Wonder-Children" as Pianists   My child of five years of age shows signs of great talent for music. He has a keen, true ear, and plays rather well for his age. Does this justify me in hoping that something out of the ordinary will become of him? They say that so-called "wonder-children" never amount to anything in later life.

That "wonder-children" never amount to anything in later life is not borne out by history. If some are disappointments it is either because they astonished by mere executive precocity, instead of

charming by their talent, or because they
were ruined by unscrupulous parents or
managers who confounded the promise
of a future with its realization. But,
aside from these few, all great musicians
were "wonder-children," whether they
became composers, pianists, violinists,
'cellists, or what not. The biographies
of our great masters of the past centuries
as well as those of more recent times
(Mendelssohn, Wagner, Chopin, Schumann, Liszt, Rubinstein, and all the
others), will bear me out in this statement.
If your child shows more than mere
precocity — if, for instance, he does not
merely play in his fifth year what others
play in their tenth, but shows qualities
of musical superiority — then you may
with a fair degree of certainty feel hopeful
of a fine musical future for him.

Shall I attend orchestra concerts or *The Value*
shall I give preference to soloists? *of Going*
to
By all means attend orchestra and *Concerts*
chamber-music concerts! For these will
acquaint you with those works which
are, after all, of the greatest importance
to the student. Besides, you will usually

hear more correct interpretations than from soloists. The latter, with some luminous exceptions, overestimate their own authority and take such unseemly liberties that in many cases you hear more Smith, Jones, or Levy than Beethoven, Schumann, or Chopin. Individuality in a soloist is certainly a great quality, but only if it is tempered by a proper deference to the composer of the work in hand. If you cannot hear a soloist who is capable of sinking his individuality in the thought, mood, and style of the composer he is interpreting — and this is given to only the very greatest — you do far better to prefer to the "individual" renditions of a soloist the "collective" renditions of the orchestra or string quartette. The synthetic nature of the orchestra forestalls the extravagances of so-called individuality and insures, generally speaking, a truthful interpretation. The very worst conductor imaginable cannot do as much harm to a composition as can a mediocre soloist, for an orchestra is a large body and, therefore, not so easily moved and shifted from the path of musical rectitude

as is a single voice or an instrument. A
really great soloist is, of course, the finest
flower of the garden of applied music,
for his touch with the instrument is
immediate and he needs no middleman
to express the finest shades of his conceptions; while the conductor — and even
the best — has to impart his conception
(through the baton, facial expression,
and gesture) to other people before it
can become audible, and on this cir-
cuitous route much of the original fervour
and ardour may be lost. But there are
more good orchestras than great soloists,
and hence you are safe in attending
orchestra and chamber-music concerts.

Compelled to study without a teacher *Books*
for two years before I can go to a con- *That Aid*
the
servatory, what method should I study *Student*
for my technique and what pieces? *Working*
Alone
You fail to say whether you are a
beginner or already somewhat advanced.
Still, I think it safe to recommend
Mason's "Touch and Technique," Stern-
berg's Etudes, opus 66; and select your
pieces from the graded catalogues which
any publisher will be glad to send you.

Music as a Profession or as an Avocation

Would you advise a young man with a good foundation to choose music — that is, concertizing — as a career, or should he keep his music as an accomplishment and avocation?

Your distinguishing between music and concertizing gives direction to my reply; that the question was not answered by your own heart before you asked it prompts me to advise music for you as an avocation. The artist's career nowadays is not so simple as it appears to be. Of a thousand capable musicians there is, perhaps, one who attains to a general reputation and fortune. The rest of them, after spending money, time, and toil, give up in despair, and with an embittered disposition take up some other occupation. If you do not depend upon public music-making for a living; if your natural endowments are not of a very unusually high order, and if your entire personality does not imply the exercise of authority over assemblages of people — spiritual authority, I mean — it were better to enjoy your music in the circle of your friends. It is less risky and will, in all probability, give you much greater satisfaction.

When I hear a concert pianist I want to get more from his playing than æsthetic ear enjoyment. Can you give me a little outline of points for which to look that may help me in my piano study?

How Much You Can Get From Music

There is no pleasure or enjoyment from which we can derive more than we bring with us in the way of receptiveness. As you deepen your study of music and gain insight into its forms, contrapuntal work and harmonic beauties you will derive more and more pleasure from listening to a good pianist the deeper your studies go. What their playing reflects of emotional life you will perceive in the exact measure of your own grasp upon life. Art is a medium connecting, like a telegraph, two stations: the sender of a message and the receiver. Both must be pitched equally high to make the communication perfect.

You would confer a favour upon a teacher by solving a problem for her that has puzzled her all her life; why do all pupils prefer flats to sharps? I am not at all sure that I do not, in some

"It is So Much Easier to Read Flats Than Sharps!"

degree, share this preference. Is it a fault of training, or has it any other cause?

Your question is both original and well justified by frequent observation, for it is quite true that people prefer to read flats to sharps. But note it well that the aversion to sharps refers only to the reading, not to the playing. If any one should find it harder to *play* in sharps, say, after knowing the notes well, it would be a purely subjective deception, due to a mental association of the note-picture with the respective sounds. My personal belief is that the aversion to the *reading* of sharps is caused by the comparative complexity of the sign itself, and this leads me to think that the whole matter belongs rather to ophthalmology than to either acoustics or music.

Rubenstein or Liszt — Which the Greater? As between Liszt and Rubinstein, whom do you consider the greater?

Rubinstein I knew very well (I was his pupil), and have heard him play a great many times. Liszt, who died when I was sixteen years old and had not

appeared in public for some twenty
years previously, I never met and
never heard. Still, from the descriptions which many of my friends gave
me of him, and from the study of his
works, I have been able to form a fair
idea of his playing and his personality.
As a virtuoso I think Liszt stood
above Rubinstein, for his playing must
have possessed amazing, dazzling qualities. Rubinstein excelled by his sincerity, by his demoniacal, Heaven-
storming power of great impassioned-
ness, qualities which with Liszt had
passed through the sieve of a superior
education and — if you understand how
I mean that term — gentlemanly elegance. He was, in the highest meaning
of the word, a man of the world;
Rubinstein, a world-stormer, with a sove-
reign disregard for conventionality and
for Mrs. Grundy. The principal difference lay in the characters of the two. As
musicians, with regard to their natural
endowments and ability, they were probably of the same gigantic calibre, such
as we would seek in vain at the present
time.

As to One Composer —Excluding All Others If I am deeply interested in Beethoven's music can I not find in him all that there is in music, in both an æsthetic and a technical sense? Is any one's music more profound?

You imagine yourself in an impenetrable stronghold whence, safe from all attacks, you may look upon all composers (except Beethoven) with a patronizing, condescending smile. But you are gravely in error. Life is too rich in experience, too many-sided in its manifestations, to permit any one master, however great, to exhaust its interpretation through his art. If you base your preference for Beethoven upon your sympathies, and if, for this reason, his music satisfies you better than that of any other composer, you are to be complimented upon your good taste. But that gives you no right to contest, for instance, the profoundness of Bach, the æsthetic charm of Chopin, the wonders of Mozart's art, nor the many and various merits of your contemporary composers. The least that one can be charged with who finds the whole of life expressed in any one composer is one-sidedness, not to speak of the fact that the understanding cannot be very deep for one master if it is closed to all others. One of the chief requirements for true connoisseurship is catholicity of taste.

I am fifty-six years old, live in the mountains sixty-five miles from any railroad, alone with my husband, and I have not taken lessons in thirty-five years. Do you think "Pischna" would help me much to regain my former ability to play? If not, what would you advise me to do?

A Sensible Scheme of Playing for Pleasure

Refrain from all especially technical work. Since your love of music is strong enough to cause you to resume your playing you should take as much pleasure in it as possible and work technically only in the pieces you play — that is, in those places which offer you difficulties. Decide upon a comfortable fingering first, and practise the difficult places separately and slowly until you feel that you can venture to play them in their appropriate speed.

*First
Learn
to Play
Simple
Things
Well*

What pieces would you advise me to memorize after Rachmaninoff's Prelude in C-sharp minor and Chopin's A-flat Ballade? These pieces do not appeal to the majority of people, but I enjoy them.

If such a work as Chopin's Ballade in A-flat does not "appeal to the majority" — as you say — the fault cannot lie in the composition, but must be sought in the interpretation. Why not try a few pieces of lesser complexity and play them so perfectly that they do appeal to the majority. Try Chopin's Nocturne, opus 27, No. 2; Schumann's Romanza, opus 28, No. 2; or his "*Traumerei*," or some of the more pretentious "Songs Without Words" by Mendelssohn.

*About
Starting
on a
Concert
Career*

I am twenty-four, have had four years' rigorous work in a conservatory and a partial college training. My technique is adequate for Brahms's Rhapsody in G minor and McDowell's Sonatas. I have good health and am determined not to grow self-satisfied. Is there a place on the concert stage — even if only as an accompanist — for a woman thus equipped?

Any public career must begin by earning the good opinion of others. One's own opinion, however just, is never a criterion. My advice is that you speak to some of the prominent concert agents, whose names and addresses you find in every well-accredited music paper. Play for them. They are usually not connoisseurs by actual knowledge, but they have developed a fine instinct for that which is of use to them, and you are, of course, aware that we must be of use to others before we can be of use to ourselves. If the right "stuff" is in you you will make your way. People of ability always do. That there is room for women on the concert stage is proved by the great array of meritorious women pianists. Especially for accompanying women are in demand — that is, for *good* accompanying. But I would not start out with the idea of accompanying. It seems like going to a commercial school to study be to an "assistant" bookkeeper. Become a fine, all-round musician, a fine pianist, and see what the tide of affairs will bring

you.   The proper level for your ability
is bound to disclose itself to you.

Accom-
panist
Usually
Precedes
Soloist
at
Entering

Should an accompanist precede or
follow the soloist on the stage in a concert
or recital, and should sex be considered
in the matter?

If the soloist be a man the accompanist
should precede him on the stage in order
to arrange his music, the height of his
seat or whatever may be necessary,
during which time the soloist salutes the
audience. For these reasons it should
be the same when the soloist is a woman,
but as women are of the feminine per-
suasion it will, perhaps, look better if
the accompanist yields precedence to her.

ALPHABETICAL INDEX OF
QUESTIONS

INDEX

A CATALOG OF SELECTED
DOVER BOOKS
IN ALL FIELDS OF INTEREST

A CATALOG OF SELECTED DOVER

BOOKS IN ALL FIELDS OF INTEREST

CONCERNING THE SPIRITUAL IN ART, Wassily Kandinsky. Pioneering work by father of abstract art. Thoughts on color theory, nature of art. Analysis of earlier masters. 12 illustrations. 80pp. of text. 5⅜ × 8½. 23411-8 Pa. $3.95

ANIMALS: 1,419 Copyright-Free Illustrations of Mammals, Birds, Fish, Insects, etc., Jim Harter (ed.). Clear wood engravings present, in extremely lifelike poses, over 1,000 species of animals. One of the most extensive pictorial sourcebooks of its kind. Captions. Index. 284pp. 9 × 12. 23766-4 Pa. $12.95

CELTIC ART: The Methods of Construction, George Bain. Simple geometric techniques for making Celtic interlacements, spirals, Kells-type initials, animals, humans, etc. Over 500 illustrations. 160pp. 9 × 12. (USO) 22923-8 Pa. $9.95

AN ATLAS OF ANATOMY FOR ARTISTS, Fritz Schider. Most thorough reference work on art anatomy in the world. Hundreds of illustrations, including selections from works by Vesalius, Leonardo, Goya, Ingres, Michelangelo, others. 593 illustrations. 192pp. 7⅛ × 10¼. 20241-0 Pa. $9.95

CELTIC HAND STROKE-BY-STROKE (Irish Half-Uncial from "The Book of Kells"): An Arthur Baker Calligraphy Manual, Arthur Baker. Complete guide to creating each letter of the alphabet in distinctive Celtic manner. Covers hand position, strokes, pens, inks, paper, more. Illustrated. 48pp. 8¼ × 11.

24336-2 Pa. $3.95

EASY ORIGAMI, John Montroll. Charming collection of 32 projects (hat, cup, pelican, piano, swan, many more) specially designed for the novice origami hobbyist. Clearly illustrated easy-to-follow instructions insure that even beginning papercrafters will achieve successful results. 48pp. 8¼ × 11. 27298-2 Pa. $2.95

THE COMPLETE BOOK OF BIRDHOUSE CONSTRUCTION FOR WOOD-WORKERS, Scott D. Campbell. Detailed instructions, illustrations, tables. Also data on bird habitat and instinct patterns. Bibliography. 3 tables. 63 illustrations in 15 figures. 48pp. 5¼ × 8½. 24407-5 Pa. $1.95

BLOOMINGDALE'S ILLUSTRATED 1886 CATALOG: Fashions, Dry Goods and Housewares, Bloomingdale Brothers. Famed merchants' extremely rare catalog depicting about 1,700 products: clothing, housewares, firearms, dry goods, jewelry, more. Invaluable for dating, identifying vintage items. Also, copyright-free graphics for artists, designers. Co-published with Henry Ford Museum & Greenfield Village. 160pp. 8¼ × 11. 25780-0 Pa. $9.95

HISTORIC COSTUME IN PICTURES, Braun & Schneider. Over 1,450 costumed figures in clearly detailed engravings—from dawn of civilization to end of 19th century. Captions. Many folk costumes. 256pp. 8⅜ × 11¼. 23150-X Pa. $11.95

STICKLEY CRAFTSMAN FURNITURE CATALOGS, Gustav Stickley and L. & J. G. Stickley. Beautiful, functional furniture in two authentic catalogs from 1910. 594 illustrations, including 277 photos, show settles, rockers, armchairs, reclining chairs, bookcases, desks, tables. 183pp. 6½ × 9¼.   23838-5 Pa. $9.95

AMERICAN LOCOMOTIVES IN HISTORIC PHOTOGRAPHS: 1858 to 1949, Ron Ziel (ed.). A rare collection of 126 meticulously detailed official photographs, called "builder portraits," of American locomotives that majestically chronicle the rise of steam locomotive power in America. Introduction. Detailed captions. xi + 129pp. 9 × 12.   27393-8 Pa. $12.95

AMERICA'S LIGHTHOUSES: An Illustrated History, Francis Ross Holland, Jr. Delightfully written, profusely illustrated fact-filled survey of over 200 American lighthouses since 1716. History, anecdotes, technological advances, more. 240pp. 8 × 10¾.   25576-X Pa. $11.95

TOWARDS A NEW ARCHITECTURE, Le Corbusier. Pioneering manifesto by founder of "International School." Technical and aesthetic theories, views of industry, economics, relation of form to function, "mass-production split" and much more. Profusely illustrated. 320pp. 6⅛ × 9¼. (USO)   25023-7 Pa. $9.95

HOW THE OTHER HALF LIVES, Jacob Riis. Famous journalistic record, exposing poverty and degradation of New York slums around 1900, by major social reformer. 100 striking and influential photographs. 233pp. 10 × 7⅞.

22012-5 Pa $10.95

FRUIT KEY AND TWIG KEY TO TREES AND SHRUBS, William M. Harlow. One of the handiest and most widely used identification aids. Fruit key covers 120 deciduous and evergreen species; twig key 160 deciduous species. Easily used. Over 300 photographs. 126pp. 5⅜ × 8½.   20511-8 Pa. $3.95

COMMON BIRD SONGS, Dr. Donald J. Borror. Songs of 60 most common U.S. birds: robins, sparrows, cardinals, bluejays, finches, more—arranged in order of increasing complexity. Up to 9 variations of songs of each species.

Cassette and manual 99911-4 $8.95

ORCHIDS AS HOUSE PLANTS, Rebecca Tyson Northen. Grow cattleyas and many other kinds of orchids—in a window, in a case, or under artificial light. 63 illustrations. 148pp. 5⅜ × 8½.   23261-1 Pa. $4.95

MONSTER MAZES, Dave Phillips. Masterful mazes at four levels of difficulty. Avoid deadly perils and evil creatures to find magical treasures. Solutions for all 32 exciting illustrated puzzles. 48pp. 8¼ × 11.   26005-4 Pa. $2.95

MOZART'S DON GIOVANNI (DOVER OPERA LIBRETTO SERIES), Wolfgang Amadeus Mozart. Introduced and translated by Ellen H. Bleiler. Standard Italian libretto, with complete English translation. Convenient and thoroughly portable—an ideal companion for reading along with a recording or the performance itself. Introduction. List of characters. Plot summary. 121pp. 5¼ × 8½.

24944-1 Pa. $2.95

TECHNICAL MANUAL AND DICTIONARY OF CLASSICAL BALLET, Gail Grant. Defines, explains, comments on steps, movements, poses and concepts. 15-page pictorial section. Basic book for student, viewer. 127pp. 5⅜ × 8½.

21843-0 Pa. $4.95

BRASS INSTRUMENTS: Their History and Development, Anthony Baines. Authoritative, updated survey of the evolution of trumpets, trombones, bugles, cornets, French horns, tubas and other brass wind instruments. Over 140 illustrations and 48 music examples. Corrected and updated by author. New preface. Bibliography. 320pp. 5⅜ × 8½. 27574-4 Pa. $9.95

HOLLYWOOD GLAMOR PORTRAITS, John Kobal (ed.). 145 photos from 1926–49. Harlow, Gable, Bogart, Bacall; 94 stars in all. Full background on photographers, technical aspects. 160pp. 8⅜ × 11¼. 23352-9 Pa. $11.95

MAX AND MORITZ, Wilhelm Busch. Great humor classic in both German and English. Also 10 other works: "Cat and Mouse," "Plisch and Plumm," etc. 216pp. 5⅜ × 8½. 20181-3 Pa. $5.95

THE RAVEN AND OTHER FAVORITE POEMS, Edgar Allan Poe. Over 40 of the author's most memorable poems: "The Bells," "Ulalume," "Israfel," "To Helen," "The Conqueror Worm," "Eldorado," "Annabel Lee," many more. Alphabetic lists of titles and first lines. 64pp. 5³⁄₁₆ × 8¼. 26685-0 Pa. $1.00

SEVEN SCIENCE FICTION NOVELS, H. G. Wells. The standard collection of the great novels. Complete, unabridged. First Men in the Moon, Island of Dr. Moreau, War of the Worlds, Food of the Gods, Invisible Man, Time Machine, In the Days of the Comet. Total of 1,015pp. 5⅜ × 8½. (USO) 20264-X Clothbd. $29.95

AMULETS AND SUPERSTITIONS, E. A. Wallis Budge. Comprehensive discourse on origin, powers of amulets in many ancient cultures: Arab, Persian, Babylonian, Assyrian, Egyptian, Gnostic, Hebrew, Phoenician, Syriac, etc. Covers cross, swastika, crucifix, seals, rings, stones, etc. 584pp. 5⅜ × 8½. 23573-4 Pa. $12.95

RUSSIAN STORIES/PYCCKNE PACCKA3bl: A Dual-Language Book, edited by Gleb Struve. Twelve tales by such masters as Chekhov, Tolstoy, Dostoevsky, Pushkin, others. Excellent word-for-word English translations on facing pages, plus teaching and study aids, Russian/English vocabulary, biographical/critical introductions, more. 416pp. 5⅜ × 8½. 26244-8 Pa. $8.95

PHILADELPHIA THEN AND NOW: 60 Sites Photographed in the Past and Present, Kenneth Finkel and Susan Oyama. Rare photographs of City Hall, Logan Square, Independence Hall, Betsy Ross House, other landmarks juxtaposed with contemporary views. Captures changing face of historic city. Introduction. Captions. 128pp. 8¼ × 11. 25790-8 Pa. $9.95

AIA ARCHITECTURAL GUIDE TO NASSAU AND SUFFOLK COUNTIES, LONG ISLAND, The American Institute of Architects, Long Island Chapter, and the Society for the Preservation of Long Island Antiquities. Comprehensive, well-researched and generously illustrated volume brings to life over three centuries of Long Island's great architectural heritage. More than 240 photographs with authoritative, extensively detailed captions. 176pp. 8¼ × 11. 26946-9 Pa. $14.95

NORTH AMERICAN INDIAN LIFE: Customs and Traditions of 23 Tribes, Elsie Clews Parsons (ed.). 27 fictionalized essays by noted anthropologists examine religion, customs, government, additional facets of life among the Winnebago, Crow, Zuni, Eskimo, other tribes. 480pp. 6⅛ × 9¼. 27377-6 Pa. $10.95

FRANK LLOYD WRIGHT'S HOLLYHOCK HOUSE, Donald Hoffmann. Lavishly illustrated, carefully documented study of one of Wright's most controversial residential designs. Over 120 photographs, floor plans, elevations, etc. Detailed perceptive text by noted Wright scholar. Index. 128pp. 9¼ × 10¾.
27133-1 Pa. $11.95

THE MALE AND FEMALE FIGURE IN MOTION: 60 Classic Photographic Sequences, Eadweard Muybridge. 60 true-action photographs of men and women walking, running, climbing, bending, turning, etc., reproduced from rare 19th-century masterpiece. vi + 121pp. 9 × 12. 24745-7 Pa. $10.95

1001 QUESTIONS ANSWERED ABOUT THE SEASHORE, N. J. Berrill and Jacquelyn Berrill. Queries answered about dolphins, sea snails, sponges, starfish, fishes, shore birds, many others. Covers appearance, breeding, growth, feeding, much more. 305pp. 5¼ × 8¼. 23366-9 Pa. $7.95

GUIDE TO OWL WATCHING IN NORTH AMERICA, Donald S. Heintzelman. Superb guide offers complete data and descriptions of 19 species: barn owl, screech owl, snowy owl, many more. Expert coverage of owl-watching equipment, conservation, migrations and invasions, etc. Guide to observing sites. 84 illustrations. xiii + 193pp. 5⅜ × 8½. 27344-X Pa. $8.95

MEDICINAL AND OTHER USES OF NORTH AMERICAN PLANTS: A Historical Survey with Special Reference to the Eastern Indian Tribes, Charlotte Erichsen-Brown. Chronological historical citations document 500 years of usage of plants, trees, shrubs native to eastern Canada, northeastern U.S. Also complete identifying information. 343 illustrations. 544pp. 6½ × 9¼. 25951-X Pa. $12.95

STORYBOOK MAZES, Dave Phillips. 23 stories and mazes on two-page spreads: Wizard of Oz, Treasure Island, Robin Hood, etc. Solutions. 64pp. 8¼ × 11.
23628-5 Pa. $2.95

NEGRO FOLK MUSIC, U.S.A., Harold Courlander. Noted folklorist's scholarly yet readable analysis of rich and varied musical tradition. Includes authentic versions of over 40 folk songs. Valuable bibliography and discography. xi + 324pp. 5⅜ × 8½. 27350-4 Pa. $7.95

MOVIE-STAR PORTRAITS OF THE FORTIES, John Kobal (ed.). 163 glamor, studio photos of 106 stars of the 1940s: Rita Hayworth, Ava Gardner, Marlon Brando, Clark Gable, many more. 176pp. 8⅜ × 11¼. 23546-7 Pa. $11.95

BENCHLEY LOST AND FOUND, Robert Benchley. Finest humor from early 30s, about pet peeves, child psychologists, post office and others. Mostly unavailable elsewhere. 73 illustrations by Peter Arno and others. 183pp. 5⅜ × 8½.
22410-4 Pa. $5.95

YEKL and THE IMPORTED BRIDEGROOM AND OTHER STORIES OF YIDDISH NEW YORK, Abraham Cahan. Film Hester Street based on Yekl (1896). Novel, other stories among first about Jewish immigrants on N.Y.'s East Side. 240pp. 5⅜ × 8½. 22427-9 Pa. $6.95

SELECTED POEMS, Walt Whitman. Generous sampling from *Leaves of Grass*. Twenty-four poems include "I Hear America Singing," "Song of the Open Road," "I Sing the Body Electric," "When Lilacs Last in the Dooryard Bloom'd," "O Captain! My Captain!"—all reprinted from an authoritative edition. Lists of titles and first lines. 128pp. 5³/₁₆ × 8¼. 26878-0 Pa. $1.00

THE BEST TALES OF HOFFMANN, E. T. A. Hoffmann. 10 of Hoffmann's most important stories: "Nutcracker and the King of Mice," "The Golden Flowerpot," etc. 458pp. 5⅜ × 8½. 21793-0 Pa. $8.95

FROM FETISH TO GOD IN ANCIENT EGYPT, E. A. Wallis Budge. Rich detailed survey of Egyptian conception of "God" and gods, magic, cult of animals, Osiris, more. Also, superb English translations of hymns and legends. 240 illustrations. 545pp. 5⅜ × 8½. 25803-3 Pa. $11.95

FRENCH STORIES/CONTES FRANÇAIS: A Dual-Language Book, Wallace Fowlie. Ten stories by French masters, Voltaire to Camus: "Micromegas" by Voltaire; "The Atheist's Mass" by Balzac; "Minuet" by de Maupassant; "The Guest" by Camus, six more. Excellent English translations on facing pages. Also French-English vocabulary list, exercises, more. 352pp. 5⅜ × 8½. 26443-2 Pa. $8.95

CHICAGO AT THE TURN OF THE CENTURY IN PHOTOGRAPHS: 122 Historic Views from the Collections of the Chicago Historical Society, Larry A. Viskochil. Rare large-format prints offer detailed views of City Hall, State Street, the Loop, Hull House, Union Station, many other landmarks, circa 1904–1913. Introduction. Captions. Maps. 144pp. 9⅜ × 12¼. 24656-6 Pa. $12.95

OLD BROOKLYN IN EARLY PHOTOGRAPHS, 1865–1929, William Lee Younger. Luna Park, Gravesend race track, construction of Grand Army Plaza, moving of Hotel Brighton, etc. 157 previously unpublished photographs. 165pp. 8⅞ × 11¾. 23587-4 Pa. $13.95

THE MYTHS OF THE NORTH AMERICAN INDIANS, Lewis Spence. Rich anthology of the myths and legends of the Algonquins, Iroquois, Pawnees and Sioux, prefaced by an extensive historical and ethnological commentary. 36 illustrations. 480pp. 5⅜ × 8½. 25967-6 Pa. $8.95

AN ENCYCLOPEDIA OF BATTLES: Accounts of Over 1,560 Battles from 1479 B.C. to the Present, David Eggenberger. Essential details of every major battle in recorded history from the first battle of Megiddo in 1479 B.C. to Grenada in 1984. List of Battle Maps. New Appendix covering the years 1967–1984. Index. 99 illustrations. 544pp. 6½ × 9¼. 24913-1 Pa. $14.95

SAILING ALONE AROUND THE WORLD, Captain Joshua Slocum. First man to sail around the world, alone, in small boat. One of great feats of seamanship told in delightful manner. 67 illustrations. 294pp. 5⅜ × 8½. 20326-3 Pa. $5.95

ANARCHISM AND OTHER ESSAYS, Emma Goldman. Powerful, penetrating, prophetic essays on direct action, role of minorities, prison reform, puritan hypocrisy, violence, etc. 271pp. 5⅜ × 8½. 22484-8 Pa. $5.95

MYTHS OF THE HINDUS AND BUDDHISTS, Ananda K. Coomaraswamy and Sister Nivedita. Great stories of the epics; deeds of Krishna, Shiva, taken from puranas, Vedas, folk tales; etc. 32 illustrations. 400pp. 5⅜ × 8½. 21759-0 Pa. $9.95

BEYOND PSYCHOLOGY, Otto Rank. Fear of death, desire of immortality, nature of sexuality, social organization, creativity, according to Rankian system. 291pp. 5⅜ × 8½. 20485-5 Pa. $8.95

A THEOLOGICO-POLITICAL TREATISE, Benedict Spinoza. Also contains unfinished Political Treatise. Great classic on religious liberty, theory of government on common consent. R. Elwes translation. Total of 421pp. 5⅜ × 8½. 20249-6 Pa. $8.95

MY BONDAGE AND MY FREEDOM, Frederick Douglass. Born a slave, Douglass became outspoken force in antislavery movement. The best of Douglass' autobiographies. Graphic description of slave life. 464pp. 5⅜ × 8½. 22457-0 Pa. $8.95

FOLLOWING THE EQUATOR: A Journey Around the World, Mark Twain. Fascinating humorous account of 1897 voyage to Hawaii, Australia, India, New Zealand, etc. Ironic, bemused reports on peoples, customs, climate, flora and fauna, politics, much more. 197 illustrations. 720pp. 5⅜ × 8½. 26113-1 Pa. $15.95

THE PEOPLE CALLED SHAKERS, Edward D. Andrews. Definitive study of Shakers: origins, beliefs, practices, dances, social organization, furniture and crafts, etc. 33 illustrations. 351pp. 5⅜ × 8½. 21081-2 Pa. $8.95

THE MYTHS OF GREECE AND ROME, H. A. Guerber. A classic of mythology, generously illustrated, long prized for its simple, graphic, accurate retelling of the principal myths of Greece and Rome, and for its commentary on their origins and significance. With 64 illustrations by Michelangelo, Raphael, Titian, Rubens, Canova, Bernini and others. 480pp. 5⅜ × 8½. 27584-1 Pa. $9.95

PSYCHOLOGY OF MUSIC, Carl E. Seashore. Classic work discusses music as a medium from psychological viewpoint. Clear treatment of physical acoustics, auditory apparatus, sound perception, development of musical skills, nature of musical feeling, host of other topics. 88 figures. 408pp. 5⅜ × 8½. 21851-1 Pa. $9.95

THE PHILOSOPHY OF HISTORY, Georg W. Hegel. Great classic of Western thought develops concept that history is not chance but rational process, the evolution of freedom. 457pp. 5⅜ × 8½. 20112-0 Pa. $9.95

THE BOOK OF TEA, Kakuzo Okakura. Minor classic of the Orient: entertaining, charming explanation, interpretation of traditional Japanese culture in terms of tea ceremony. 94pp. 5⅜ × 8½. 20070-1 Pa. $3.95

LIFE IN ANCIENT EGYPT, Adolf Erman. Fullest, most thorough, detailed older account with much not in more recent books, domestic life, religion, magic, medicine, commerce, much more. Many illustrations reproduce tomb paintings, carvings, hieroglyphs, etc. 597pp. 5⅜ × 8½. 22632-8 Pa. $10.95

SUNDIALS, Their Theory and Construction, Albert Waugh. Far and away the best, most thorough coverage of ideas, mathematics concerned, types, construction, adjusting anywhere. Simple, nontechnical treatment allows even children to build several of these dials. Over 100 illustrations. 230pp. 5⅜ × 8½. 22947-5 Pa. $7.95

DYNAMICS OF FLUIDS IN POROUS MEDIA, Jacob Bear. For advanced students of ground water hydrology, soil mechanics and physics, drainage and irrigation engineering, and more. 335 illustrations. Exercises, with answers. 784pp. 6⅛ × 9¼. 65675-6 Pa. $19.95

SONGS OF EXPERIENCE: Facsimile Reproduction with 26 Plates in Full Color, William Blake. 26 full-color plates from a rare 1826 edition. Includes "The Tyger," "London," "Holy Thursday," and other poems. Printed text of poems. 48pp. 5¼ × 7. 24636-1 Pa. $4.95

OLD-TIME VIGNETTES IN FULL COLOR, Carol Belanger Grafton (ed.). Over 390 charming, often sentimental illustrations, selected from archives of Victorian graphics—pretty women posing, children playing, food, flowers, kittens and puppies, smiling cherubs, birds and butterflies, much more. All copyright-free. 48pp. 9¼ × 12¼. 27269-9 Pa. $5.95

PERSPECTIVE FOR ARTISTS, Rex Vicat Cole. Depth, perspective of sky and sea, shadows, much more, not usually covered. 391 diagrams, 81 reproductions of drawings and paintings. 279pp. 5⅜ × 8½. 22487-2 Pa. $6.95

DRAWING THE LIVING FIGURE, Joseph Sheppard. Innovative approach to artistic anatomy focuses on specifics of surface anatomy, rather than muscles and bones. Over 170 drawings of live models in front, back and side views, and in widely varying poses. Accompanying diagrams. 177 illustrations. Introduction. Index. 144pp. 8⅜ × 11¼. 26723-7 Pa. $8.95

GOTHIC AND OLD ENGLISH ALPHABETS: 100 Complete Fonts, Dan X. Solo. Add power, elegance to posters, signs, other graphics with 100 stunning copyright-free alphabets: Blackstone, Dolbey, Germania, 97 more—including many lower-case, numerals, punctuation marks. 104pp. 8⅛ × 11. 24695-7 Pa. $8.95

HOW TO DO BEADWORK, Mary White. Fundamental book on craft from simple projects to five-bead chains and woven works. 106 illustrations. 142pp. 5⅜ × 8. 20697-1 Pa. $4.95

THE BOOK OF WOOD CARVING, Charles Marshall Sayers. Finest book for beginners discusses fundamentals and offers 34 designs. "Absolutely first rate . . . well thought out and well executed."—E. J. Tangerman. 118pp. 7¾ × 10⅝. 23654-4 Pa. $5.95

ILLUSTRATED CATALOG OF CIVIL WAR MILITARY GOODS: Union Army Weapons, Insignia, Uniform Accessories, and Other Equipment, Schuyler, Hartley, and Graham. Rare, profusely illustrated 1846 catalog includes Union Army uniform and dress regulations, arms and ammunition, coats, insignia, flags, swords, rifles, etc. 226 illustrations. 160pp. 9 × 12. 24939-5 Pa. $10.95

WOMEN'S FASHIONS OF THE EARLY 1900s: An Unabridged Republication of "New York Fashions, 1909," National Cloak & Suit Co. Rare catalog of mail-order fashions documents women's and children's clothing styles shortly after the turn of the century. Captions offer full descriptions, prices. Invaluable resource for fashion, costume historians. Approximately 725 illustrations. 128pp. 8⅜ × 11¼. 27276-1 Pa. $11.95

THE 1912 AND 1915 GUSTAV STICKLEY FURNITURE CATALOGS, Gustav Stickley. With over 200 detailed illustrations and descriptions, these two catalogs are essential reading and reference materials and identification guides for Stickley furniture. Captions cite materials, dimensions and prices. 112pp. 6½ × 9¼. 26676-1 Pa. $9.95

EARLY AMERICAN LOCOMOTIVES, John H. White, Jr. Finest locomotive engravings from early 19th century: historical (1804–74), main-line (after 1870), special, foreign, etc. 147 plates. 142pp. 11⅜ × 8¼. 22772-3 Pa. $10.95

THE TALL SHIPS OF TODAY IN PHOTOGRAPHS, Frank O. Braynard. Lavishly illustrated tribute to nearly 100 majestic contemporary sailing vessels: Amerigo Vespucci, Clearwater, Constitution, Eagle, Mayflower, Sea Cloud, Victory, many more. Authoritative captions provide statistics, background on each ship. 190 black-and-white photographs and illustrations. Introduction. 128pp. 8⅞ × 11¾. 27163-3 Pa. $13.95

EARLY NINETEENTH-CENTURY CRAFTS AND TRADES, Peter Stockham (ed.). Extremely rare 1807 volume describes to youngsters the crafts and trades of the day: brickmaker, weaver, dressmaker, bookbinder, ropemaker, saddler, many more. Quaint prose, charming illustrations for each craft. 20 black-and-white line illustrations. 192pp. 4⅝ × 6. 27293-1 Pa. $4.95

VICTORIAN FASHIONS AND COSTUMES FROM HARPER'S BAZAR, 1867–1898, Stella Blum (ed.). Day costumes, evening wear, sports clothes, shoes, hats, other accessories in over 1,000 detailed engravings. 320pp. 9⅜ × 12¼.
22990-4 Pa. $13.95

GUSTAV STICKLEY, THE CRAFTSMAN, Mary Ann Smith. Superb study surveys broad scope of Stickley's achievement, especially in architecture. Design philosophy, rise and fall of the Craftsman empire, descriptions and floor plans for many Craftsman houses, more. 86 black-and-white halftones. 31 line illustrations. Introduction. 208pp. 6½ × 9¼. 27210-9 Pa. $9.95

THE LONG ISLAND RAIL ROAD IN EARLY PHOTOGRAPHS, Ron Ziel. Over 220 rare photos, informative text document origin (1844) and development of rail service on Long Island. Vintage views of early trains, locomotives, stations, passengers, crews, much more. Captions. 8⅞ × 11¾. 26301-0 Pa. $13.95

THE BOOK OF OLD SHIPS: From Egyptian Galleys to Clipper Ships, Henry B. Culver. Superb, authoritative history of sailing vessels, with 80 magnificent line illustrations. Galley, bark, caravel, longship, whaler, many more. Detailed, informative text on each vessel by noted naval historian. Introduction. 256pp. 5⅜ × 8½. 27332-6 Pa. $6.95

TEN BOOKS ON ARCHITECTURE, Vitruvius. The most important book ever written on architecture. Early Roman aesthetics, technology, classical orders, site selection, all other aspects. Morgan translation. 331pp. 5⅜ × 8½. 20645-9 Pa. $8.95

THE HUMAN FIGURE IN MOTION, Eadweard Muybridge. More than 4,500 stopped-action photos, in action series, showing undraped men, women, children jumping, lying down, throwing, sitting, wrestling, carrying, etc. 390pp. 7⅞ × 10⅝.
20204-6 Clothbd. $24.95

TREES OF THE EASTERN AND CENTRAL UNITED STATES AND CANADA, William M. Harlow. Best one-volume guide to 140 trees. Full descriptions, woodlore, range, etc. Over 600 illustrations. Handy size. 288pp. 4½ × 6⅜.
20395-6 Pa. $5.95

SONGS OF WESTERN BIRDS, Dr. Donald J. Borror. Complete song and call repertoire of 60 western species, including flycatchers, juncoes, cactus wrens, many more—includes fully illustrated booklet. Cassette and manual 99913-0 $8.95

GROWING AND USING HERBS AND SPICES, Milo Miloradovich. Versatile handbook provides all the information needed for cultivation and use of all the herbs and spices available in North America. 4 illustrations. Index. Glossary. 236pp. 5⅜ × 8½. 25058-X Pa. $6.95

BIG BOOK OF MAZES AND LABYRINTHS, Walter Shepherd. 50 mazes and labyrinths in all—classical, solid, ripple, and more—in one great volume. Perfect inexpensive puzzler for clever youngsters. Full solutions. 112pp. 8⅛ × 11.
22951-3 Pa. $4.95

PIANO TUNING, J. Cree Fischer. Clearest, best book for beginner, amateur. Simple repairs, raising dropped notes, tuning by easy method of flattened fifths. No previous skills needed. 4 illustrations. 201pp. 5⅜ × 8½. 23267-0 Pa. $5.95

A SOURCE BOOK IN THEATRICAL HISTORY, A. M. Nagler. Contemporary observers on acting, directing, make-up, costuming, stage props, machinery, scene design, from Ancient Greece to Chekhov. 611pp. 5⅜ × 8½. 20515-0 Pa. $11.95

THE COMPLETE NONSENSE OF EDWARD LEAR, Edward Lear. All nonsense limericks, zany alphabets, Owl and Pussycat, songs, nonsense botany, etc., illustrated by Lear. Total of 320pp. 5⅜ × 8½. (USO) 20167-8 Pa. $6.95

VICTORIAN PARLOUR POETRY: An Annotated Anthology, Michael R. Turner. 117 gems by Longfellow, Tennyson, Browning, many lesser-known poets. "The Village Blacksmith," "Curfew Must Not Ring Tonight," "Only a Baby Small," dozens more, often difficult to find elsewhere. Index of poets, titles, first lines. xxiii + 325pp. 5⅜ × 8¼. 27044-0 Pa. $8.95

DUBLINERS, James Joyce. Fifteen stories offer vivid, tightly focused observations of the lives of Dublin's poorer classes. At least one, "The Dead," is considered a masterpiece. Reprinted complete and unabridged from standard edition. 160pp. 5³⁄₁₆ × 8¼. 26870-5 Pa. $1.00

THE HAUNTED MONASTERY and THE CHINESE MAZE MURDERS, Robert van Gulik. Two full novels by van Gulik, set in 7th-century China, continue adventures of Judge Dee and his companions. An evil Taoist monastery, seemingly supernatural events; overgrown topiary maze hides strange crimes. 27 illustrations. 328pp. 5⅜ × 8½. 23502-5 Pa. $7.95

THE BOOK OF THE SACRED MAGIC OF ABRAMELIN THE MAGE, translated by S. MacGregor Mathers. Medieval manuscript of ceremonial magic. Basic document in Aleister Crowley, Golden Dawn groups. 268pp. 5⅜ × 8½.
23211-5 Pa. $8.95

NEW RUSSIAN-ENGLISH AND ENGLISH-RUSSIAN DICTIONARY, M. A. O'Brien. This is a remarkably handy Russian dictionary, containing a surprising amount of information, including over 70,000 entries. 366pp. 4½ × 6⅛.
20208-9 Pa. $9.95

HISTORIC HOMES OF THE AMERICAN PRESIDENTS, Second, Revised Edition, Irvin Haas. A traveler's guide to American Presidential homes, most open to the public, depicting and describing homes occupied by every American President from George Washington to George Bush. With visiting hours, admission charges, travel routes. 175 photographs. Index. 160pp. 8¼ × 11. 26751-2 Pa. $10.95

NEW YORK IN THE FORTIES, Andreas Feininger. 162 brilliant photographs by the well-known photographer, formerly with *Life* magazine. Commuters, shoppers, Times Square at night, much else from city at its peak. Captions by John von Hartz. 181pp. 9¼ × 10¾. 23585-8 Pa. $12.95

INDIAN SIGN LANGUAGE, William Tomkins. Over 525 signs developed by Sioux and other tribes. Written instructions and diagrams. Also 290 pictographs. 111pp. 6⅛ × 9¼. 22029-X Pa. $3.50

ANATOMY: A Complete Guide for Artists, Joseph Sheppard. A master of figure drawing shows artists how to render human anatomy convincingly. Over 460 illustrations. 224pp. 8⅜ × 11¼. 27279-6 Pa. $10.95

MEDIEVAL CALLIGRAPHY: Its History and Technique, Marc Drogin. Spirited history, comprehensive instruction manual covers 13 styles (ca. 4th century thru 15th). Excellent photographs; directions for duplicating medieval techniques with modern tools. 224pp. 8⅜ × 11¼. 26142-5 Pa. $11.95

DRIED FLOWERS: How to Prepare Them, Sarah Whitlock and Martha Rankin. Complete instructions on how to use silica gel, meal and borax, perlite aggregate, sand and borax, glycerine and water to create attractive permanent flower arrangements. 12 illustrations. 32pp. 5⅜ × 8½. 21802-3 Pa. $1.00

EASY-TO-MAKE BIRD FEEDERS FOR WOODWORKERS, Scott D. Campbell. Detailed, simple-to-use guide for designing, constructing, caring for and using feeders. Text, illustrations for 12 classic and contemporary designs. 96pp. 5⅜ × 8½. 25847-5 Pa. $2.95

OLD-TIME CRAFTS AND TRADES, Peter Stockham. An 1807 book created to teach children about crafts and trades open to them as future careers. It describes in detailed, nontechnical terms 24 different occupations, among them coachmaker, gardener, hairdresser, lacemaker, shoemaker, wheelwright, copper-plate printer, milliner, trunkmaker, merchant and brewer. Finely detailed engravings illustrate each occupation. 192pp. 4⅝ × 6. 27398-9 Pa. $4.95

THE HISTORY OF UNDERCLOTHES, C. Willett Cunnington and Phyllis Cunnington. Fascinating, well-documented survey covering six centuries of English undergarments, enhanced with over 100 illustrations: 12th-century laced-up bodice, footed long drawers (1795), 19th-century bustles, 19th-century corsets for men, Victorian "bust improvers," much more. 272pp. 5⅜ × 8¼. 27124-2 Pa. $9.95

ARTS AND CRAFTS FURNITURE: The Complete Brooks Catalog of 1912, Brooks Manufacturing Co. Photos and detailed descriptions of more than 150 now very collectible furniture designs from the Arts and Crafts movement depict davenports, settees, buffets, desks, tables, chairs, bedsteads, dressers and more, all built of solid, quarter-sawed oak. Invaluable for students and enthusiasts of antiques, Americana and the decorative arts. 80pp. 6½ × 9¼. 27471-3 Pa. $7.95

HOW WE INVENTED THE AIRPLANE: An Illustrated History, Orville Wright. Fascinating firsthand account covers early experiments, construction of planes and motors, first flights, much more. Introduction and commentary by Fred C. Kelly. 76 photographs. 96pp. 8¼ × 11. 25662-6 Pa. $8.95

THE ARTS OF THE SAILOR: Knotting, Splicing and Ropework, Hervey Garrett Smith. Indispensable shipboard reference covers tools, basic knots and useful hitches; handsewing and canvas work, more. Over 100 illustrations. Delightful reading for sea lovers. 256pp. 5⅜ × 8½. 26440-8 Pa. $7.95

FRANK LLOYD WRIGHT'S FALLINGWATER: The House and Its History, Second, Revised Edition, Donald Hoffmann. A total revision—both in text and illustrations—of the standard document on Fallingwater, the boldest, most personal architectural statement of Wright's mature years, updated with valuable new material from the recently opened Frank Lloyd Wright Archives. "Fascinating"—*The New York Times.* 116 illustrations. 128pp. 9¼ × 10¾. 27430-6 Pa. $10.95

PHOTOGRAPHIC SKETCHBOOK OF THE CIVIL WAR, Alexander Gardner. 100 photos taken on field during the Civil War. Famous shots of Manassas, Harper's Ferry, Lincoln, Richmond, slave pens, etc. 244pp. 10⅝ × 8¼.
22731-6 Pa. $9.95

FIVE ACRES AND INDEPENDENCE, Maurice G. Kains. Great back-to-the-land classic explains basics of self-sufficient farming. The one book to get. 95 illustrations. 397pp. 5⅜ × 8½. 20974-1 Pa. $7.95

SONGS OF EASTERN BIRDS, Dr. Donald J. Borror. Songs and calls of 60 species most common to eastern U.S.: warblers, woodpeckers, flycatchers, thrushes, larks, many more in high-quality recording. Cassette and manual 99912-2 $8.95

A MODERN HERBAL, Margaret Grieve. Much the fullest, most exact, most useful compilation of herbal material. Gigantic alphabetical encyclopedia, from aconite to zedoary, gives botanical information, medical properties, folklore, economic uses, much else. Indispensable to serious reader. 161 illustrations. 888pp. 6½ × 9¼. 2-vol. set. (USO) Vol. I: 22798-7 Pa. $9.95
Vol. II: 22799-5 Pa. $9.95

HIDDEN TREASURE MAZE BOOK, Dave Phillips. Solve 34 challenging mazes accompanied by heroic tales of adventure. Evil dragons, people-eating plants, bloodthirsty giants, many more dangerous adversaries lurk at every twist and turn. 34 mazes, stories, solutions. 48pp. 8¼ × 11. 24566-7 Pa. $2.95

LETTERS OF W. A. MOZART, Wolfgang A. Mozart. Remarkable letters show bawdy wit, humor, imagination, musical insights, contemporary musical world; includes some letters from Leopold Mozart. 276pp. 5⅜ × 8½. 22859-2 Pa. $7.95

BASIC PRINCIPLES OF CLASSICAL BALLET, Agrippina Vaganova. Great Russian theoretician, teacher explains methods for teaching classical ballet. 118 illustrations. 175pp. 5⅜ × 8½. 22036-2 Pa. $4.95

THE JUMPING FROG, Mark Twain. Revenge edition. The original story of The Celebrated Jumping Frog of Calaveras County, a hapless French translation, and Twain's hilarious "retranslation" from the French. 12 illustrations. 66pp. 5⅜ × 8½.
22686-7 Pa. $3.95

BEST REMEMBERED POEMS, Martin Gardner (ed.). The 126 poems in this superb collection of 19th- and 20th-century British and American verse range from Shelley's "To a Skylark" to the impassioned "Renascence" of Edna St. Vincent Millay and to Edward Lear's whimsical "The Owl and the Pussycat." 224pp. 5⅜ × 8½.
27165-X Pa. $4.95

COMPLETE SONNETS, William Shakespeare. Over 150 exquisite poems deal with love, friendship, the tyranny of time, beauty's evanescence, death and other themes in language of remarkable power, precision and beauty. Glossary of archaic terms. 80pp. 5³/₁₆ × 8¼. 26686-9 Pa. $1.00

BODIES IN A BOOKSHOP, R. T. Campbell. Challenging mystery of blackmail and murder with ingenious plot and superbly drawn characters. In the best tradition of British suspense fiction. 192pp. 5⅜ × 8½. 24720-1 Pa. $5.95

THE WIT AND HUMOR OF OSCAR WILDE, Alvin Redman (ed.). More than 1,000 ripostes, paradoxes, wisecracks: Work is the curse of the drinking classes; I can resist everything except temptation; etc. 258pp. 5⅜ × 8½. 20602-5 Pa. $5.95

SHAKESPEARE LEXICON AND QUOTATION DICTIONARY, Alexander Schmidt. Full definitions, locations, shades of meaning in every word in plays and poems. More than 50,000 exact quotations. 1,485pp. 6½ × 9¼. 2-vol. set.
Vol. I: 22726-X Pa. $16.95
Vol. 2: 22727-8 Pa. $15.95

SELECTED POEMS, Emily Dickinson. Over 100 best-known, best-loved poems by one of America's foremost poets, reprinted from authoritative early editions. No comparable edition at this price. Index of first lines. 64pp. 5³⁄₁₆ × 8¼.
26466-1 Pa. $1.00

CELEBRATED CASES OF JUDGE DEE (DEE GOONG AN), translated by Robert van Gulik. Authentic 18th-century Chinese detective novel; Dee and associates solve three interlocked cases. Led to van Gulik's own stories with same characters. Extensive introduction. 9 illustrations. 237pp. 5⅜ × 8½.
23337-5 Pa. $6.95

THE MALLEUS MALEFICARUM OF KRAMER AND SPRENGER, translated by Montague Summers. Full text of most important witchhunter's "bible," used by both Catholics and Protestants. 278pp. 6⅝ × 10. 22802-9 Pa. $11.95

SPANISH STORIES/CUENTOS ESPAÑOLES: A Dual-Language Book, Angel Flores (ed.). Unique format offers 13 great stories in Spanish by Cervantes, Borges, others. Faithful English translations on facing pages. 352pp. 5⅜ × 8½.
25399-6 Pa. $8.95

THE CHICAGO WORLD'S FAIR OF 1893: A Photographic Record, Stanley Appelbaum (ed.). 128 rare photos show 200 buildings, Beaux-Arts architecture, Midway, original Ferris Wheel, Edison's kinetoscope, more. Architectural emphasis; full text. 116pp. 8¼ × 11. 23990-X Pa. $9.95

OLD QUEENS, N.Y., IN EARLY PHOTOGRAPHS, Vincent F. Seyfried and William Asadorian. Over 160 rare photographs of Maspeth, Jamaica, Jackson Heights, and other areas. Vintage views of DeWitt Clinton mansion, 1939 World's Fair and more. Captions. 192pp. 8⅞ × 11. 26358-4 Pa. $12.95

CAPTURED BY THE INDIANS: 15 Firsthand Accounts, 1750–1870, Frederick Drimmer. Astounding true historical accounts of grisly torture, bloody conflicts, relentless pursuits, miraculous escapes and more, by people who lived to tell the tale. 384pp. 5⅜ × 8½. 24901-8 Pa. $8.95

THE WORLD'S GREAT SPEECHES, Lewis Copeland and Lawrence W. Lamm (eds.). Vast collection of 278 speeches of Greeks to 1970. Powerful and effective models; unique look at history. 842pp. 5⅜ × 8½. 20468-5 Pa. $14.95

THE BOOK OF THE SWORD, Sir Richard F. Burton. Great Victorian scholar/adventurer's eloquent, erudite history of the "queen of weapons"—from prehistory to early Roman Empire. Evolution and development of early swords, variations (sabre, broadsword, cutlass, scimitar, etc.), much more. 336pp. 6⅛ × 9¼. 25434-8 Pa. $8.95

CATALOG OF DOVER BOOKS

AUTOBIOGRAPHY: The Story of My Experiments with Truth, Mohandas K. Gandhi. Boyhood, legal studies, purification, the growth of the Satyagraha (nonviolent protest) movement. Critical, inspiring work of the man responsible for the freedom of India. 480pp. 5⅜ × 8½. (USO) **24593-4 Pa. $8.95**

CELTIC MYTHS AND LEGENDS, T. W. Rolleston. Masterful retelling of Irish and Welsh stories and tales. Cuchulain, King Arthur, Deirdre, the Grail, many more. First paperback edition. 58 full-page illustrations. 512pp. 5⅜ × 8½. **26507-2 Pa. $9.95**

THE PRINCIPLES OF PSYCHOLOGY, William James. Famous long course complete, unabridged. Stream of thought, time perception, memory, experimental methods; great work decades ahead of its time. 94 figures. 1,391pp. 5⅜ × 8½. 2-vol. set.
Vol. I: **20381-6 Pa. $12.95**
Vol. II: **20382-4 Pa. $12.95**

THE WORLD AS WILL AND REPRESENTATION, Arthur Schopenhauer. Definitive English translation of Schopenhauer's life work, correcting more than 1,000 errors, omissions in earlier translations. Translated by E. F. J. Payne. Total of 1,269pp. 5⅜ × 8½. 2-vol. set.
Vol. 1: **21761-2 Pa. $11.95**
Vol. 2: **21762-0 Pa. $11.95**

MAGIC AND MYSTERY IN TIBET, Madame Alexandra David-Neel. Experiences among lamas, magicians, sages, sorcerers, Bonpa wizards. A true psychic discovery. 32 illustrations. 321pp. 5⅜ × 8½. (USO) **22682-4 Pa. $8.95**

THE EGYPTIAN BOOK OF THE DEAD, E. A. Wallis Budge. Complete reproduction of Ani's papyrus, finest ever found. Full hieroglyphic text, interlinear transliteration, word-for-word translation, smooth translation. 533pp. 6½ × 9¼. **21866-X Pa. $9.95**

MATHEMATICS FOR THE NONMATHEMATICIAN, Morris Kline. Detailed, college-level treatment of mathematics in cultural and historical context, with numerous exercises. Recommended Reading Lists. Tables. Numerous figures. 641pp. 5⅜ × 8½. **24823-2 Pa. $11.95**

THEORY OF WING SECTIONS: Including a Summary of Airfoil Data, Ira H. Abbott and A. E. von Doenhoff. Concise compilation of subsonic aerodynamic characteristics of NACA wing sections, plus description of theory. 350pp. of tables. 693pp. 5⅜ × 8½. **60586-8 Pa. $14.95**

THE RIME OF THE ANCIENT MARINER, Gustave Doré, S. T. Coleridge. Doré's finest work; 34 plates capture moods, subtleties of poem. Flawless full-size reproductions printed on facing pages with authoritative text of poem. "Beautiful. Simply beautiful."—*Publisher's Weekly*. 77pp. 9¼ × 12. **22305-1 Pa. $6.95**

NORTH AMERICAN INDIAN DESIGNS FOR ARTISTS AND CRAFTSPEOPLE, Eva Wilson. Over 360 authentic copyright-free designs adapted from Navajo blankets, Hopi pottery, Sioux buffalo hides, more. Geometrics, symbolic figures, plant and animal motifs, etc. 128pp. 8⅜ × 11. (EUK) **25341-4 Pa. $7.95**

SCULPTURE: Principles and Practice, Louis Slobodkin. Step-by-step approach to clay, plaster, metals, stone; classical and modern. 253 drawings, photos. 255pp. 8⅛ × 11. **22960-2 Pa. $10.95**

THE INFLUENCE OF SEA POWER UPON HISTORY, 1660–1783, A. T. Mahan. Influential classic of naval history and tactics still used as text in war colleges. First paperback edition. 4 maps. 24 battle plans. 640pp. 5⅜ × 8½.
25509-3 Pa. $12.95

THE STORY OF THE TITANIC AS TOLD BY ITS SURVIVORS, Jack Winocour (ed.). What it was really like. Panic, despair, shocking inefficiency, and a little heroism. More thrilling than any fictional account. 26 illustrations. 320pp. 5⅜ × 8½.
20610-6 Pa. $8.95

FAIRY AND FOLK TALES OF THE IRISH PEASANTRY, William Butler Yeats (ed.). Treasury of 64 tales from the twilight world of Celtic myth and legend: "The Soul Cages," "The Kildare Pooka," "King O'Toole and his Goose," many more. Introduction and Notes by W. B. Yeats. 352pp. 5⅜ × 8½.
26941-8 Pa. $8.95

BUDDHIST MAHAYANA TEXTS, E. B. Cowell and Others (eds.). Superb, accurate translations of basic documents in Mahayana Buddhism, highly important in history of religions. The Buddha-karita of Asvaghosha, Larger Sukhavativyuha, more. 448pp. 5⅜ × 8½. ,
25552-2 Pa. $9.95

ONE TWO THREE . . . INFINITY: Facts and Speculations of Science, George Gamow. Great physicist's fascinating, readable overview of contemporary science: number theory, relativity, fourth dimension, entropy, genes, atomic structure, much more. 128 illustrations. Index. 352pp. 5⅜ × 8½.
25664-2 Pa. $8.95

ENGINEERING IN HISTORY, Richard Shelton Kirby, et al. Broad, nontechnical survey of history's major technological advances: birth of Greek science, industrial revolution, electricity and applied science, 20th-century automation, much more. 181 illustrations. ". . . excellent . . ."—Isis. Bibliography. vii + 530pp. 5⅜ × 8¼.
26412-2 Pa. $14.95

Prices subject to change without notice.

Available at your book dealer or write for free catalog to Dept. GI, Dover Publications, Inc., 31 East 2nd St., Mineola, N.Y. 11501. Dover publishes more than 500 books each year on science, elementary and advanced mathematics, biology, music, art, literary history, social sciences and other areas.